CURRENTS
IN THE
ELECTRIC
CITY

CURRENTS IN THE ELECTRIC CITY

A SCRANTON ANTHOLOGY

EDITED BY
BRIAN FANELLI
AND JOE KRAUS

Belt Publishing

First Edition 2024
ISBN: 978-1-953368-77-5

Belt Publishing
6101 Penn Avenue, Suite 201, Pittsburgh PA 15206
www.beltpublishing.com

Cover by David Wilson

TABLE OF CONTENTS

Foreword
Joe Kraus...ix

Introduction
Brian Fanelli...1

Bringing the World to Scranton
Sondra Myers 3

Not from Here
Maria Johnson..5

Two Poems by John (Jack) E. McGuigan..........................11

Introduction to the Dunmore Cemetery Tour
Julie Esty..15

Two Poems by Bonita Lini Markowski 17

Dear Scranton
Daryl Fanelli...19

Outage in the Electric City
Jade Williams..21

Escape Plan
Amye Archer...27

Two Poems by Laurel Radzieski 31

Train Lady
Julie Esty..35

Little Miss Know-It-All
Barbara J. Taylor..37

Enjoying a Smoke in Scranton
Stephanie Longo 47

A Ted of Two Cities
Ted LoRusso 51

The Five Seasons of Scranton
Thomas Kielty Blomain..57

Phylum Familia Immigrandorum
Andrea Talarico 61

Three Poems by Gerard Grealish............................67

The Indian American Dream
Janvi Patel..71

Reclamation
Pauline Palko..77

The House in the Hills
Lizzy Ke Polishan 79

Three Poems by David Elliott..................................83

Scranton the City, Scranton Myself
Maureen McGuigan 87

Violet
Julie Esty...91

Two Poems by Scott Thomas....................................93

Three Poems by Susan Luckstone Jaffer...............97

Dedicated to the Venues That Raised Me
Jess Meoni 101

City Noise
Dimitri Bartels-Bray 105

song of the city electric
Alicia Grega 109

The House on Frink Street
Dawn Leas 113

From the Classroom to the Chaos
Tom Borthwick 115

Two Poems by Brian Fanelli 119

What Washed Windows Can Do
Mandy Pennington 121

Scranton from the Pipes
Chris Newell 127

The Miner
Julie Esty 131

**When in Week Six a Student Spoke
of Her Roommate's Father's Death**
John Meredith Hill 133

**Palimpsest of Scranton, or
Scranton in the American Popular Imagination**
Joe Kraus 135

Contributors 141

Foreword

JOE KRAUS

I first heard about the Belt City Series when friends of mine contributed to the Chicago anthology, *Rust Belt Chicago*, in 2017. And I thought, Why not Scranton? Couldn't we bring together the voices of different Scranton writers to produce a book that would celebrate what Scranton is, was, and will be?

I wanted to be a part of any such project, but I confess my bona fides were thin. I work in Scranton—I'm a professor at "da U"—but I don't live here. I drive in every workday, and I explore the city on many a lunch hour, but it's not *mine* in the way it is for most of the contributors here.

The piece I've contributed, "Palimpsest of Scranton, or Scranton in the American Popular Imagination," grows out of my sense of partial outsider-ness. It's my exploration of how others have seen Scranton from the outside, and it draws on my now two-decades-old collection of favorite quotes about our Electric City.

But as I explored how to make this collection come together—having received encouragement from Belt publisher Anne Trubek—I realized I couldn't do it without a *real* Scrantonian.

I "met" Brian Fanelli the way you're supposed to meet people in Scranton—first by reputation, then through his family, and finally in person. The reputation part came when I read—and admired—his poetry collection *Waiting for the Dead to Speak*. The family part came when his niece, Jessica, did an independent study with me. And in person, well, I asked if he'd consider being a part of the project, and he said yes. It's Scranton, and there's a basic sense of trust that undergirds that kind of question.

This book doesn't happen without Brian, without his sensibility or his love of the city and its people.

Fortunately, Brian and I share an admiration for authenticity, for writers speaking in their own voices, for writers pushing the "rules" of writing ever so slightly.

We share a belief as well in what the Belt City Anthology series represents: that the voice of the city is a chorus, not a solo. Decades ago,

Scranton was famous as a stop on the vaudeville circuit, and you can still hear the refrain, "If you can play Scranton, you can play anywhere," as a lingering sign of that history.

That word, "vaudeville"—at least as I understand it—is a corruption of the French phrase, *voix du ville*, literally "the voice of the city." Vaudeville functioned by bringing a series of performances across a single stage, giving one performer after another the chance to sing a song, tell a joke, dance, recount a story, perform a magic trick, or present an oddity.

Our stage in this book is smaller than the great theaters of that era, but the thinking is the same. We present here a variety of poems, essays, and dramatic monologues by and about the people of Scranton. Our contributors come with different experiences as writers and with different experiences of the city, but they all share a sense that, as they speak for themselves, they speak as well for the city as a whole.

Raise the curtain, then, and please join us in reading what our fellow Scrantonians have to offer as they represent, critique, and celebrate the city we share.

Introduction

BRIAN FANELLI

I grew up in a tiny yellow house in north Scranton, where my parents somehow raised five children. Yes, I shared a bedroom, and so we didn't melt during muggy Pennsylvania summers, my brother and I ran a window AC held together by duct tape. Sometimes, it worked. Other times, it roared to life and then sputtered out. If we gave it a good whack, it would often chug along and eventually keep us cool. With the AC cranked, I lay in bed, beneath a *Return of the Jedi* poster, wondering what existed beyond my insular north Scranton neighborhood.

During my senior year of high school, I was sure of one thing: I wanted to ditch Northeastern Pennsylvania. Hello, Philly area. I stayed there for a few years following college graduation and worked full-time at a daily newspaper. Everyone, yes everyone, in the newsroom assumed people from Scranton were like Dwight from *The Office*, no matter how many times I told them that wasn't the case. Why did I feel the burning need to defend the place I wanted to leave? Why did I care what wealthy Philadelphia suburbanites thought? Perhaps I relished the role of feeling like an underdog in that place and sticking up for my scrappy hometown.

Whether I wanted to admit it or not, Scranton left its mark on me like coal dust. Even though I said I'd never return, I eventually moved back home and have long since secured a decent full-time job and a place within the local arts and literary community. When coeditor Joe Kraus asked me to help with this project, I immediately said yes, in hopes that maybe, just maybe, it would give a new perspective to the Electric City.

As the writing in this anthology illustrates, Scranton is a multifaceted place with a long and complicated history. Many of the pieces celebrate the city's past and specific childhood memories, including Tom Blomain's "The Five Seasons of Scranton," Dawn Leas's "The House on Frink Street," and Jack McGuigan's "How I Learned to Run."

While some of the work acknowledges the difficulty of living in Scranton, such as Amye Archer's "Escape Plan" and Jade Williams's "Outage in the Electric City," others highlight the positives. I specifically relate to Jess Meoni's "Dedicated to the Venues That Raised Me." I know those music clubs, places like Café del Sol, Test Pattern, and Café Metropolis (OK, that was in Wilkes-Barre, but still). I pogoed and slam danced on those sticky floors and had two-hour-long conversations with high school friends about getting out of town. Though I can't relate to what it's like to be a woman in the punk scene, I know exactly what she means by the importance of those venues and how they can forge a worldview and turn a sixteen-year-old with spiky hair into an activist. Unfortunately, those clubs are all gone, but by writing that essay, Meoni honors them and what those five-dollar shows meant to kids living in a place with not much else to do.

This anthology also contains unique perspectives on familiar Scranton landmarks and businesses. Mandy Pennington's "What Washed Windows Can Do" gives a personal take on the Steamtown Mall and its many changes. Stephanie Longo uses her journalistic skills to showcase the story behind Parodi Cigar Group and thus, a broader immigrant narrative, while Scott Thomas's poem "On Seeing Louie in a Toadstool" explores family history and the promise that the lights of Lackawanna Station meant in 1938.

It took me a long time to figure out my relationship to Scranton and the fact I'm a native. Sometimes, I still have the itch to escape and often hop in my car to return to Philly, but I've made peace with the city, and I'm eager to see its next phase. As you'll see from this anthology, many of the writers have a genuine affection for Scranton, economic challenges and all. I count myself among those that want to see the Electric City succeed, which is part of the reason I signed on with this anthology.

What I hope this anthology proves is that Scranton is more than a faux documentary TV series about a paper company, a John Mitchell labor rights statue at Courthouse Square, or an election stop every midterm and presidential cycle. Yes, we gave birth to a president, but we're more than a political slogan or punchline. Joe and I are grateful to Belt Publishing for allowing us to add Scranton to their city anthology series. Despite its challenges, the city is evolving, trying its hardest to be more than coal mine tours and President Biden's hometown. In the spirit of the writers that once called this place home, including Pulitzer Prize–winning playwright Jason Miller and Pulitzer Prize–winning poet W. S. Merwin, we present to you an anthology about Scranton. I promise that there's only one or two pieces that mention *The Office*.

Bringing the World to Scranton

SONDRA MYERS

First and foremost, Scranton is a city. It's not a town, and most important, it's not a suburb.

I spent the first ten years in Old Forge—which is a workingman's town. A number of coal miners and people recovering from their days in the mines lived there.

My mother was from Philadelphia—she met my dad when he was at law school at Penn. When my mother's siblings came to visit—she was the youngest of nine—they assured her that the door back home would be open for her whenever she was ready to move back into civilization.

My father's law practice was in Scranton, and when I was ten, we moved here.

My own work through the years took me to Harrisburg, with frequent assignments in Philadelphia. From there, it was off to Washington, where I took a job with the chair of the National Endowment for the Humanities.

I value diversity, and here, I found it in the Hill Section.

History: In my school, James Madison, there were Catholics, Protestants, and Jews, and—unique to our town—African Americans. I can't resist saying that Ulysses Robinson, a Black kid who lived with his grandmother in the Lower Hill, was the best student in our class from day one. He went on to be valedictorian in high school and was accepted at Harvard, Yale, and Princeton. He chose Yale.

Here is another passion of mine: the quality of arts education. There should not be a lower standard for people who live in smaller communities. One of the reasons that I loved the Metropolitan Opera films is that people everywhere could have that excellent experience. I thought that the Met Opera president should be given a Nobel Prize for that.

Coming back here from Washington was something of a struggle, but when I saw some of Scranton's assets—both its people and its institutions—I knew, as Joe Biden knew of our country, that it was a place of possibilities.

Not from Here

MARIA JOHNSON

"How can you *possibly* not have heard of him?" my eldest daughter's boyfriend asked her in our kitchen one afternoon, about six months into their relationship. The him in question, Bob Sura, was a local guy who went on to play ten seasons in the NBA and is a really big deal in these parts.

"Babe, you gotta remember I'm not actually from here?"

"OK, fair point."

Made perfect sense to them. Thing is, by any normal standards she *is* from here: born at Community Medical Center up by the park, lived here all her life. But her parents aren't from here, and in Scranton, if your parents, and your grandparents, and your aunts and uncles and cousins aren't from here, you will never be really From Here.

When my husband and I moved here for my job at the University (called "da U," if you are from here) my new colleagues warned us that this is what it would be like: If you're not From Here, they told me, you'll always be an outsider. People are nice enough, they said, but it's really provincial and honestly a little bit inbred, and you'll probably never make it beyond the fringes. University social life tends to be a bit incestuous too, they said. We outsiders generally stick together.

Some questions:

First, who *is* from here? Well, really, the Lenape, the Munsee, the Shawnee, and the Susquehannock. But unsurprisingly, that's not what people tend to mean. They mean the Irish, Welsh, Italians, Poles, Lithuanians, and Russians whose ancestors came here to work the anthracite mines and steel mills and garment factories, and the English (mainly) who owned and ran the mines and mills and factories, back when the valley was a major industrial center and Scranton had the first electric trolley system in the US. Their descendants (and not the Jews or the Black people who came around the same time) are what people mean when they say From Here. I am not from here, and therefore my kids are not From Here, despite here being the place they are from.

Another question: Where is *here*?

One answer: *here* is "NEPA"—it's an abbreviation for Northeast PA, but it's a word, too: "NEE-pa"—the string of towns that stretch "up da line" from Scranton to Carbondale—Dunmore, Throop, Olyphant, Peckville, Archbald—and "down da line" to Wilkes-Barre—Old Forge, Taylor, Moosic, Pittston. Makes sense up to a point. But people often mean something more specific. Our very first day, as we were unloading the moving truck, an elderly couple on a morning walk stopped to chat. We asked, "So are you from around here?" "Oh no," they said, "We're from Wilkes-Barre." Now Wilkes-Barre is all of twenty-five minutes away, but they "got back" only once or twice a year.

So, another approach: *here* is the city/township/borough itself. For us, that's Scranton. If you turn right out of our front steps and walk four blocks, you will leave Scranton and enter Dunmore. You'd never notice the difference, but if you're from Dunmore, it's a huge deal. Another conversation—an appendix to the "You're not from here, are you? Where are you from?" conversation—goes like this: "Oh that's nice, so where do you live?" "Monroe." Pause. "What block?" "The 8" (that's how you say it here—we're on the 8 of Monroe, the 4 of Quincy, etc.). Pause. "So that's . . . (pause) . . . Scranton?" "Yup." Faint expression crosses the face of my interlocutor—pity, disdain, and even a hint of suspicion, blended into an emotion highly specific to people from Dunmore encountering people from Scranton.

Third way of looking at it: *here* is the neighborhood. The couple next door grew up on the West Side and moved in a couple of weeks after we did. They are migrants, too, like the couple from Wilkes-Barre or that you would be if you moved three blocks from Dunmore to Scranton, except that would *never* happen. This is the approach I have personally adopted to the "where is here" question. I can be snooty and superior about provincial attitudes to Wilkes-Barre or Dunmore, but I am a passionate partisan of the Hill Section. It's something of a joke among my friends. "You're moving to Clarks Summit? You know Maria will never speak to you again, right?" When we are interviewing new outsiders to join us here, my colleagues always ask the candidate, "Has Maria given you the Hill speech yet?" and the candidate, magically in on the joke despite having only set foot in Scranton six hours earlier, says, "Oh, she certainly did!" and knowing glances are exchanged. OK. Fine. If someone decides they want to live in Clarks Summit (it's a suburb, people—not even a real place) perhaps I *do* make the sort of face Dunmore people do when they learn I live on "the 8." But you know what? I've been involved in hiring most of my colleagues, and most of them live on the Hill. And it's pretty great. Our kids can walk to each other's houses, and there are plenty of parties. Should the grown-ups ever have cause to decide that driving from one is not a great idea, they can just walk home and come back in the morning for the car. The few who live somewhere other than the Hill? Outsiders. Never see 'em. They generally don't get invited because they are not, you know, from here.

So here we are—"here" meaning the Hill, "we" meaning overlapping clusters of other people who are neither from here nor From Here but are here now and some of whom have become, effectively, family. If a kid asks me who's coming for dinner this Sunday and I'll say, "It'll just be the family," they will know to expect adults from New Jersey, Massachusetts, Scotland, Minnesota, Texas, and—our closest approximation to a local—Allentown, with children who are from here/not From Here and each others' *de facto* cousins (their "real" cousins being in Italy, South Carolina, Mexico, etc.). A bigger event will include people who started in Long Island, Ireland, Wyoming, Kansas, Utah, Louisiana, and so on, passed through various institutions of higher learning, and wound up taking jobs at da U.

That's one circle of fellow outsiders. Another has nothing to do with da U but belongs to a community of the kind of Orthodox Jews with big black hats and *peyahs* and *tzitzits*, who moved here to escape Brooklyn rents—they tend toward huge families, and in the Hill, you can get a seven bedroom with a yard for the price of a parking space in Crown Heights. As a rule, they keep to themselves, but once I had persuaded Ahuva from four doors down that I could be trusted not to let her kids eat anything if she let them come over, our children became inseparable. My kids grew up yammering about *mitzvot* and *Sheva Brachas* and *upsherin*, and arguing staunchly that beans aren't kosher (yes they are, and anyways, we're Catholic. Eat your beans). Over the years, we've been in lots of places that *goyim* rarely go—brisses and bar mitzvahs and weddings (fact: Orthodox Jewish weddings are simply the most fun it is possible to have) and dinners in *sukkahs* wearing four layers of clothes with rain dripping into the soup. Last wedding we were at, a matchmaker pestered the mother of the bride for our contact details; my daughters had caught the eye of several young men, she said, and the families wanted to make contact. My friend had a hard job persuading her that, contrary to appearances, they were not *at all* what the lady or her clients were looking for. The girls may stick out as being Not From Here but can effortlessly fool a professional into thinking they are likely in the market for a nice *frum* boy.

Some of the neighborhood Jews are more extravagantly not from here. Through a complicated story involving a man just around the corner who sells violins from his house and whose son sobbed unrestrainedly (in a good and *highly* contagious way) throughout his wedding to Esty from four-doors-down, Scranton has become a hub for converts to Orthodoxy from Latin America. Esty's high school graduation was full of girls with names like Shulamit Garcia and Batsheva Lopez. The supernice lady across the street, who is expecting her nth baby any day now, and who regularly and somewhat mysteriously gives us wholesale-size boxes of nonkosher food for our parish's pantry, is half Chinese, and her husband is Puerto Rican, I think.

Actually, if you narrow the definition of "here" *way* the heck down to "our block," most of us aren't from here in any sense at all. We have had neighbors from Central and South America, India and Indonesia and Syria. For a couple of summers, the climbing frame in our backyard was a tangle of exuberant kids from the DRC. The Congolese only stayed a few years before moving on to cities with bigger communities, but the Lhotshampa (from Nepal and then Bhutan and then back to Nepal, which decided they were no longer From There and put them in horrible refugee camps) have settled in. There's a community center and a couple of restaurants and a community garden on the corner of our block and an old guy who walks up and down the street in a Dhaka topi and a T-shirt that says "Irish Grandma," and some younger guys with extravagant haircuts and lots of kids who always knock on the back door and ask very politely if they can play on the climbing frame. The newest arrivals are from Afghanistan—we will have to wait and see if they settle here or, like the Congolese, move on.

When we first got here and they told us we would never belong, it didn't bother me. My father was born in Italy, my mother in Mississippi, and I grew up in Scotland. I'm used to not really being from anywhere, to knowing that wherever I am, there is a kind of belonging, a bone-deep knowledge of how things are, that takes several generations to acquire and that is simply not accessible to me. Swaddled as I am in all sorts of privilege—educational, racial, economic—I've never really found it uncomfortable to be an outsider. And honestly, everyone's insistence that, try as we might, we would never break through gave me a welcome excuse not to even try. So I have followed my natural inclination—cowardice, laziness, snobbery, call it what you will: this is an excuse, not a justification—and have pretty much stuck with my fellow outsiders and dodged the parish committees and PTAs and boards and other worthy civic activities where I could put my multiple privileges to work for the greater good but where everybody is married to everybody else's second cousin or have been friends since they were in tap class or Little League forty years back and where my Not-From-Hereness would be thrown into high relief. I'm not proud of it, but it's the truth.

There *was* one way, they told us, that you can break through into belonging, and that is if your kids "marry in" and you acquire a tangle of in-laws. I didn't quite believe them, but weirdly enough, it actually seems to work—a Not-From-Here woman who married into a big local family actually got elected goshdarn *mayor*. Boyfriend-of-Eldest has the kind of unimpeachable From Here credentials that entitle him to scoff at my daughter's ignorance of local sports legends. His great-grandparents were all either born in the valley or settled here as immigrants from Poland and Italy, and when not nerding out about literary fiction or rock guitar or rules of evidence, he can—and this is a crucial mark of From-Here-ness—discuss with nuance and passion, and at remarkable length, the various genres, subgenres, and microgenres of local pizza. Of course, I don't know what the future holds. I would sooner eat an entire tray (that's what it's called here) from Moroni's with American cheese (no, I'm not kidding, and yes, it's *horrible*) than come over all "So what are your intentions, young man?" But they've been together for going on four years now, so there may be hope for us yet.

Two Poems by John (Jack) E. McGuigan

How I Learned to Run

My college didn't have a track
team and cross-country had another
twenty years before its introduction,
so my formal running career spanned
only five seasons, 8th to 12th grade.

Because no other sport fit the rhythms,
the beat, of my working-class world, I ran
in English measures, just for fun:
The 180-yard low hurdles, the 440-yard dash.

I qualified for States at University Park
in my junior and senior years, ran a leg
of the mile relay and finished fifth.

Growing up in North Scranton,
we played on culm dumps (piles
of coal dust or slack;
small pieces of anthracite,
impure anthracite,
shale), ran on chunky, loose rock.

We ran on this shale,
this silt as soft as sand, sank
up to our ankles in it, and we learned to drop
our arms and let momentum scare us
down the hills.

Every kid had a mother whose voice
was a starter's gun that shocked the air
when supper neared, or when it was time
to end a game of Hooper or Kick the Can.
Their voices like breakers'
whistles sent us racing for home. Racing
Against a different clock.

Part of a Geography Gilbert Street

The lower end of Greenridge Street was dirt
From Rockwell to the coal dump;
one side was lined with nine clapboard
houses (all with porches and front yards

filled with trees and flowers
whose names we had yet to learn).
On late autumn mornings
Thin layers of wrinkled ice

Covered the potholes like cellophane.
Twice each summer oil trucks sprayed the block,
Petroleum odors replaced dust.
We had to invent clever ways of crossing

To the other side where mountains
Of white ash offered a maze of paths
And trails for us to follow while imagining
The stories of mine mules grazing

Beneath us in dark underground pastures
Beyond Sueta's house lay the ruins
Of the Legget's Creek Mine.
Huge culm piles, taller than anything

We'd known, stood like sentries
Guarding a past whose history
We heard in the coughing and wheezing
That echoed in our dark tunneled hallways,

Late into the night.
We climbed them in every weather
And stood higher than the world,
Saw through wisps of smoke:

The small street,
The little houses,
Everything changing.

Introduction to the Dunmore Cemetery Tour

JULIE ESTY

Spending decades in a cemetery is not something people want to do while they're alive. It certainly was not my plan. It happened in little bits over years and years. My affiliation with the Dunmore Cemetery began in the 1970s. Despite going to Central High School, I attended the football games at Dunmore High School. All those years ago, there was a route to get into the football stadium by going through surrounding cemeteries. If I sneaked into the cemetery and didn't pay admission, that would have afforded me seventy-five cents to buy a pack of cigarettes. Certainly not one of my prouder moments.

When the 1980s came along, I spent countless hours in the Dunmore Cemetery practicing photography. My photography teacher was horrified by my photos. At that point, cemetery photography was not the accepted genre it is today. Despite the teacher not approving of what I did, the Dunmore Cemetery was the perfect place to learn. No one there was going anywhere, so if I made a mistake, I could always go back and reshoot. That was when I started to memorize who was buried in the cemetery and where they were located. A little Rolodex formed in my head. I couldn't imagine all those years ago that the information would be used twenty years in the future.

At that time, I was also working at one of the local hospitals as a transcriptionist in Medical Records and X-Ray. By the mid- to late eighties, I'd had enough. I'd typed too many medical reports that didn't have good outcomes. I was afraid of death. I was young. I left out of fear. Look at where I ended up!

In the 1990s, I exchanged my camera for a reproduction of a Civil War–era dress. I started doing educational programs for schools and social organizations. Tours in the cemetery were an offering of the Lackawanna Historical Society, so I joined them. When they changed formats and opted out of cemetery walking tours, I took over tours in the cemetery.

I assembled an all-volunteer troupe of actors now known as the Dearly Departed Players.

For almost twenty years, under my direction, together, we have brought the Dunmore Cemetery to life by portraying people buried there. The Dunmore Cemetery Tour is now one of Northeastern Pennsylvania's most anticipated annual happenings. Every October, hundreds of people assemble at the gates of this city of the dead to not only hear stories from the past but to join us in a celebration of life and hope.

It has been an honor these many years to portray and tell the stories of the people of Northeastern Pennsylvania. Every person, from the richest to the poorest, was a beautiful thread in the magnificent tapestry of the Lackawanna Valley. The scripts for three of them are included in this anthology.

In all these years, one thing I've learned about cemeteries is that they are a lot like libraries. Every person buried in them is an amazing book. It's my job to open the books and tell the stories.

From time to time, people ask me if I will ever stop doing tours in the Dunmore Cemetery. I've been out there for forty some years. I'm sixty-two years old. I think I can do another forty! Looking forward to it!

Two Poems by Bonita Lini Markowski

Labor Day: The Electric City

I watch the night sky—
My eye fixed on Time and Space
hanging just above the Electric City sign.
I can't see the stars, so I invite
the neon to replace them   still
I see only dark, the hungry mouth
of the mines. It's Labor Day.   I think,
no one here has forgotten the coal.
Young or old it's plaited into their DNA,
specks of it still in my own knees.
We drink a beer or two conscious
that tomorrow, we will labor the day
away in blue black resignation.

What the Plants Hear

On Prescott Street there was
a pear tree in the backyard—
behind it, a couple of drunks
in a tumble-down house.
Their icy voices, every night,
would ramble & drop onto the fiesta
of portulacas that clambered
over the cinder blocks separating
yard from yard. In the evenings
I would sit on the back porch feeling
embarrassed as they dragged me
into the intimacy of their hate.
      One night, as the sun dropped,
my stomach tied knots
—a revelation—
my neighbors, the plants too, could hear
my parents cursing God & each other—
the disharmony fleeing through the clapboard,
clawing through asphalt shingles, growing
with the lilacs—I wondered
If, in the shifting of night winds, the murder
of words, would finally perch in the pear tree
with the relentless crows pecking
at the ripening fruit. For what did I know
about what plants could hear? What did I know
of this place I called home?

Dear Scranton

DARYL FANELLI

We've given you everything.
We sacrifice our rust-bottomed cars to your potholes.
Our children to your broken school system.
Our livers to your bars & boredom to your streets.
We've given you our jobs, our money, the lungs of our ancestors.
What else could you possibly need to change your ugly ways?
How can we open your empty storefronts?
What can we do to warm you like your coffee shops
in winter? We want to protect you. Want to embrace you
like hot bearskin so you don't freeze to death.
We want your rooftop park in summer.
Give us the town our grandparents remember.
Be the Globe at Christmas, but all year long.
Reduce your rent and stop closing your schools.
Lower your taxes so important people stick around.
We need shrinks at the VA and better dentists.
We need you to scare off the mob and corrupt politicians.
Why is your water brown? Give us water we can drink.
Fight back against those who toss beer cans in your flower beds.
Give us a safe place to listen for the hum of electricity,
the buzz of innovation sizzling in the street.
Give us innovation. Give us that 20th century hope in the 21st century.
We want the fire of the labor movement. Can you give us that flame?
If you can't give us that, at least save yourself
from those who don't know you.
Never sell out. Never transfer ownership.
Give your people permission to choose how you die.
Let us hack you to pieces and build homes for our homeless.
Let us clean up your courthouse and close your prisons.
Let us kill your mall once and for all and plant trees in the rubble.
Give us a wall and we'll finger paint murals for our kids.
Untie our hands and empower us to illustrate your story.

Outage in the Electric City

JADE WILLIAMS

"I'm not even from here." Born in Newark, New Jersey, my migration to Scranton at the age of three seemed a personal affront. By age twelve, Scranton was synonymous with casual alcoholism and mediocrity, and most of my tween fantasies included driving away from whatever Section 8–approved apartment my family was living in that year with the ideal soundtrack for escape (cue "Rearview Mirror" by Pearl Jam).

In true Du Boisian style, I split in two. Scranton-me was a delicate balance of ambition and apathy—AP student with a proclivity for recreational substances and three-hour depression naps. She was the picture of chill, never ruffled by a Black joke or casual misogyny, sardonically honest about the cockroach palace she called home and the sometimes cruel, sometimes lovely addict she called her mother. All the while, my "true" self waited for the time—and more importantly the place—where she could shine with all the grace and rage dancing behind the "veil." I wouldn't need to reinvent myself—just reveal myself and breathe.

I romanticized my disdain for the town. It was a textured recipe for resentment: typical teen angst coupled with the reality of being a poor Black girl in a town that often seemed to forget it was home to poor Black girls too. I thought that hating Scranton not only made me nihilistically cool but guaranteed my eventual triumphant departure. In the interim, I spent blurred days in the passenger seat of friends' cars. After hotboxing someone's mom's minivan, I would suppress the weed-induced panic by pressing my face against the window, watching dense canopies of changing leaves whirl by on Snake Road. I spent aimless days blowing cigarette smoke into thick summer air, legs dangling over Step Falls or hooking up with boys in woods they knew better than I ever could, trying to reconcile how the beauty of mountains and ice-stained rocks could exist in a place like this.

I knew that, unlike many of my peers, I didn't have the money or connections to get out of the Hill Section, so I relied on grade grubbing and my inexplicable likeability among the Scranton High School faculty as my one-way ticket to an almost mythical elsewhere. However, books threatened my strategic detachment, and I found myself losing hours of daylight in the Albright Memorial Library, subsisting off the dollar bars of Gertrude Hawk chocolate eternally displayed at the front desk. I applied to work at the library despite knowing the same people worked there since I was five and would probably die stacking books in the YA section. I ended up working at the Auntie Anne's in the historic Steamtown Mall after school instead, which by this time was less a mall and more an accumulation of misfit businesses—a gym, a dentist, a tax office, a patchouli-scented craft store, Boscov's, and a few straggling staples of modern American malls.

My first and forever favorite job consisted of rolling pretzels, reading on sacks of flour during my mandated-for-minors breaks, and supplying elderly mall walkers with mediocre coffee because they refused to go to the Starbucks downstairs. My coworkers made you forget you were working, and we formed the bonds grown only in the condensed stress of the service industry—bonds forged defending one another against the inevitable abuse of an entitled customer, laughing at the strange requests of regulars, and oversharing in the lulls between. The wage of $7.25 an hour was not much, but everything I earned was mine and not subject to the late-night demands of my mother when her sober generosity turned into inebriated desperation. She still sometimes asked for a short-term loan for an even shorter-term high, but I was able to refuse.

My school began buzzing with the prospect of college applications and the dizzying transition out of compulsory education. The Career Resource Center consisted of one woman for approximately two thousand students, so I was effectively on my own. This woman persuaded everyone to apply to the University of Scranton as a "backup," announcing loudly that free lunch recipients like me got their application fees waived, so no harm in trying.

After a rushed common app submission and a flowery personal statement, I got into all the schools I applied to with some presidential scholarships that I could humblebrag about on Facebook. I decided on Fordham the instant I opened the blood-red folder, and I immediately started planning all the bold NYC outfits I would wear on my brisk walks to class. I would get box braids and learn to walk in high-heeled boots. I would pay the ghastly $15 for cigarettes and share them only with interesting-looking people. I would go to museums with my impossibly diverse group of friends and debate the merit of long-dead artists. I would take my grandmother to shows when she visited on weekends and watch as her furrowed brow softened. I would return for holidays and find my mother sober and unbearably beautiful, the way I strained to remember her.

I didn't know about enrollment fees or housing deposits. I didn't know that every step of the process required financial verification, proof that you were the type who should even consider college. An insurmountable seven hundred dollars stood between me and escape. My grandmother searched for solutions but ultimately ended the discussion with the pained expression I had known all my life, the one that said how hard she tried, how she wished she could do more even though it was never her job to do anything. The dream ended as quickly as it had begun. The University of Scranton required only $150 to enroll. With the right timing, I could compel the money from my mother before it disappeared in a pipe. When the deadline and her disability check came, she said, "Wait for tomorrow." I frantically explained how admissions offices don't accept IOUs, how today was the last day, how she had promised. She reluctantly handed over the money. I'll never know if it was my damp eyelashes or the fact that most students don't come an hour before closing with an envelope of cash, but the bursar told me to keep it, handed me a gray Royals T-shirt, and said, "Welcome to Scranton."

I was irrevocably fucked. Another four years of Italian festivals, of St. Patrick's Day Parades, of ugly chain restaurants where people dined in sweatpants, of coffee dates with high school friends I never liked, of Friday night joyrides as the only activity after 8:00 p.m., of home and all that came with it.

Despite living next to it my entire life, I knew little about the University of Scranton. I knew that students crossed Mulberry Street with an abandon reserved for the extremely privileged, and my grandmother called them "golden feet" whenever we almost hit one on our way downtown. I knew that their dining hall held the only Chick-fil-A in town, but none of the "townies" would breach the threshold to try it. I knew that my older sister had chosen to go there two years before and seemed happy—testament to how fundamentally different we were. I learned very little at summer orientation, as a spirited sophomore from upstate New York showed us around a campus I had used as a scenic shortcut.

Life hardly changed for me, until it did. I spent my second semester smoking and reading outside Weinberg Memorial Library or smoking and reading outside Moses Taylor Hospital, where my mother frequented as her body found new ways to die. Internal bleeding, medically induced coma, liver failure, seizures—it didn't matter, she never stayed long. Until she did.

She left our house for the final time at 2:00 a.m. late that spring. From two floors away, I heard her groans and asked if she wanted to go to the emergency room. For the first time in months, she did not fight, yell, or joke away concern. She silently asked for help getting dressed. I climbed into the ambulance as she looked for the last time at her home of ten years washed in red and blue light, this house whose hardened carpets held everything she ever spilled (beer, herself, etc.), this house she shared with the woman who brought her into the world and the people she had accidentally brought into hers.

I stayed up all night as she folded in on herself; the gruff exterior of a woman who took no shit couldn't hold out against the turbulence of a body determined to quit. I overheard a presumably racist nurse complain to a cluster of white women sipping Dunkin iced coffees about my mother's quiet pleas for something for the pain, and I lost it. I screamed in her face, trying to convince her, and probably myself, that my mother had value, that she deserved peace.

I spent summer break visiting my forty-three-year-old mother in a nursing and rehabilitation center in Dunmore, and no one would just say she was dying. But a month later, she did. For such a small woman, she had always taken up so much space, and somehow, her absence seemed to take up more. It sucked the air out of the entire city and replaced it with the scent of frankincense and myrrh.

Part of my compulsion to leave Scranton was to get away from her, but I never imagined she'd beat me to the punch, leaving me with her unboxed ashes. She never liked the town either and often reminded us that we did not belong here, regaling us with stories about who she was before we came and who she would be if we ever left. I didn't realize until she was gone that she had been leaving the whole time—quick hazy trips that required only twenty bucks and a lighter or just the cheapest malt. In one of her final lucid conversations, my grandmother asked if she knew where she was. She spouted off street names and parks near a hospital in New Jersey with a clarity and confidence that almost convinced me we were there. It seemed like we had given up on the idea of leaving Scranton around the same time.

I stayed the next five years. The first three made me almost forget I had ever wanted to leave. The last two made me wonder how I had survived the other twenty.

I graduated college with no plans except to spend three months in Japan with a man I had fallen in love with, and when I returned, the only thing waiting for me was exactly what I had left behind. I floated from one soul-crushing job to the next, doing yoga in the bathrooms to keep from screaming. Two days at Macy's, five months at a local bank, one year at a nonprofit. I spent days slipping into autopilot, driving to and from work wondering how I got there. I told everyone I was planning to go to graduate school, but I never really knew if that was true; I just needed something to say.

My arms started going numb, eye-sockets throbbing, vision blurring, head pulsating on the brink of explosion. Doctors said migraines, but I was convinced that my brain had begun to atrophy from months of filling out deposit slips and bingeing Yuengling, so I decided to apply to grad school. After months of GREs, writing samples, letters of recommendations, and explaining to my boss I had never planned to stay, spring came with the intimidating promise of decisions—a forgotten luxury and burden.

I decided on the University of Illinois Urbana-Champaign, despite an unappealing campus visit at the tail end of a midwestern polar vortex. By the end of the summer, after an almost twenty-year delay, I would be moving eight hundred miles from Scranton. In the meantime, I looked for apartments online with my partner. We paid the security deposit for a one bedroom in a bright blue half-double on a street named Eureka. We sold my 2003 Elantra, knowing it would never make the trip, certain any public transit had to be better than the Colts buses. We plotted how to drive thirteen hours in a rented minivan with my elderly cat. We attended a quintessential Scranton "going away" with cornhole, disinterested strangers, and Bud Light. We saved what we could from answering phones and bussing tables and hoped it would be enough.

Around 11:30 p.m. on a balmy August night, we packed the minivan with all the clothes, books, and plates that could fit, as well as a lamp I had thrifted with my grandmother years before. I lingered on the porch, smoking a cigarette, praying it would never go out, knowing that waking up in a strange place without familiar laughter might not be worth it. But I felt the enlarged cherry of the finished cigarette warm the flesh between my fingers, and I had to stub it out.

There was no exultant score in the background, no elegantly hostile march to the car while my enemies watched, no sunshine cascading down my back as I flipped off the Welcome to Scranton sign, no mother to feel conflicted about walking away from. There was my grandmother and my siblings, waving in unison like a patch of overgrown grass, and tears streaming down my face all the way to I-81 and a yelping twenty-two-pound cat in my lap and a selfless, caffeinated man asking me to plug our new address into the GPS.

Nearly four years, a global pandemic, and three-quarters of a PhD program later, I still accidentally call Scranton home. I've lived in three apartments, bought more furniture than I know what to do with, and changed my driver's license. Illinois should be my home, but it doesn't have Yuengling or Sicilian pizza or a single fucking mountain or blizzards or the weird stuffed birds in the Everhart Museum.

You never really leave home; you just find new ways to fit into it like a worn sweater that changes shape every time you wash it. Home fits me loose now, stretched out around the neck and sleeves from years of anxious pulling, but much more comfortable. It will never be my favorite piece of clothing, it's much too stained and familiar, but it's durable, and I've never lost it in a move.

Escape Plan

AMYE ARCHER

"Cause if we don't leave this town, we might never make it out."

1987:

My father is offered a job in Orlando. The memory is fuzzy for me. I am ten, and I remember our household being thrown into chaos. In my version, my mother doesn't want to move to Florida. My older sister and I very much do. Even then, I longed for somewhere else. There's a phone call, and my father takes it in their bedroom. I listen outside the door. Or maybe I hear this afterward. Or maybe I never hear it at all. My father is offered a job as an animator at Disney. A fact he later clarifies as not being as secure as it sounds. Still, we do not go. And a root begins to form at my feet, connecting me to Scranton.

1994:

I become obsessed with the West Coast. My high school English teacher reads us a story about a town in Oregon where artisans blow glass baubles and plant them in the brown, grainy sand for beachcombers to find. The Pacific laps at the shoreline as families scour the dunes for these treasures. My first husband, who was only a boyfriend at the time, shuts down any talk of going west. Instead, we spend warm summer nights in his tiny bedroom playing video games. I am seventeen. I can't go to the West Coast alone. My insides are made of cotton candy, and standing up against the tide feels impossible. Those roots tangle between my chubby toes.

2000:

My first husband, a fiancé by this time, agrees to interview for an insurance company in Philly. I have an English degree. My fiancé is jobless and schoolless. We drive my small Geo Metro two and a half hours south to interview with a company willing to hire us both to sell insurance and pay us just enough to live in this city. It's a cold, gray day. The air is pregnant with the next dousing of rain, and we are in the parking lot screaming at one another. He will not take the job, not leave home, not leave his bedroom, not move forward. He knows I will not leave without him. That night, he cries in the dark about how sorry he is and how he is ruining my life. He suffers from panic disorder and horrible anxiety. Moving two hours south feels like a world away to him. I pull him into my chest and whisper, "I'm exactly where I want to be." The thickening roots tickling the back of my throat.

2002:

I am a manager at a local television station. Against everyone's better judgment, I have married my first husband. We were married only days before the attacks on 9/11 and watched the towers collapse from our hotel room on our honeymoon. I introduced him to the ocean on that trip, hoped it would call to him like she calls to me every time I see her. A West Coast station tries to poach me. They are in California and are willing to pay me next to nothing to come out and work for them. I don't even ask him. I turn them down. But not before I cry myself to sleep four nights in a row, considering all the ways I can abandon my life and run. My thin, cheap wedding band is a root holding me here.

2005:

I am divorced. For the first time in my adult life, I have no one and nothing to care for. I feel thin, I feel young, and I feel effortless, rootless as I walk through the world. My only sister has moved to New York City, and I make plans to follow. Over drinks one night, my father—who paid happily for my divorce—offers me seed money to relocate after I sob about how badly I need to leave this town. I will leave in the fall, I tell myself, after our busiest season at work. Two weeks later, I meet my second husband. Within a month, he moves in, and within a year, we are married and expecting twins. A pair of roots tangle in my pregnant belly.

2013:

My husband is a carpenter. He works early and long and hard. His palms are calloused and caked with roughness. I am home with our girls building a teaching career. I teach part-time at what feels like ten different schools for shit pay. I have no insurance, not even a paid parking spot. That summer, the union work dries up. The stress on our little family feels heavy and dark. I decide it's time to make another run for the West Coast. Seattle is as good a place as any. She offers moody skies and open minds. We put our house on the market and prepare our families. Our daughters are six now and think this is a great adventure. Then, I am offered a job I cannot turn down. A good job with good benefits and free tuition for my girls. Later that year, we break ground for the house my husband will build us with his bare hands. A large machine digs away the earth, roots and all.

2022:

It is a warm, summer day in July. I stand on the porch watching hummingbirds sip sugar water from our new feeder. The sun rises over the tree line to the south. The sky is magnificent, red bleeding into purple, bleeding into orange, melting into yellow and blue. Our dogs, two border collies, run circles on the sixty acres surrounding us, around the pear and maple trees we planted the year we moved in. We live fifteen minutes north of Scranton now, the furthest I have ever lived from her in my adult life. In recent years, I have come to understand her. Maybe even accept her. Through therapy, I have worked through many of our issues and have come to accept the good things she has given me. The strong work ethic, the free-range childhood, a strong family history forged in her coal mines. I am who I am because of her or despite her. I have stopped trying to escape. For now.

I sip my coffee before I sit down and begin my day working from home as a writer. Our girls, now sophomores, will get their own ride home from school, spend ten minutes at home before leaving again. I will spend the late afternoon in our garden gathering food for dinner. I harvest and prune and dig my palms deep into the dirt, careful not to disturb the roots.

Two Poems by Laurel Radzieski

Everything I Forgot about Scranton

The name of the important train.
The name of the playwright.
The name of the other playwright.
Where Test Pattern was.
Where New Visions was.
When the last issue of *Electric City* came out.
Which Coney Island had the best hot dogs.
Which Coney Island had the best fries.
Why not to drink the green beer.
Why the treehouse closed.
Why the zoo closed.
Why all the schools closed.
The reason everyone was mad at the school board.
The reason everyone was mad at the city council.
The reason everyone was mad at the mayor.
Where the bus route changed.
Where the street signs changed.
Where that stop sign used to be.

Presidential Town Hall, Scranton, March 5, 2020

There was horse shit in the street.
Mounted officers wore sunglasses.
There was a barricade,
a crowd outside the gates.
My ticket got me a wristband.
The crowd wore red, blue, white.
The protesters were a block or two away.
I felt like I was going to a concert.
My ticket could have got me more.
I had been invited to sit on the stage,
in view, behind the President.
I declined, was not behind the President.
When I got in the theater I sat
high up in a seat at the back,
but was soon beckoned in,
sandwiched between
a group of biker veterans and two teens
who had been waved in
decked out in flag windbreakers, red hats.
The teenagers were happy.
The bikers were happy.
Everyone was happy.
We sat, 700, body next to body,
ten days before.
The President joked,
told us not to worry
about some virus.
He told us life was good.
When I left, there was more
horse shit in the street.

I went to a bar to drink
with a group of women who had protested.
Their posterboard signs
leaned against a wall.
One woman's debit card was rejected.
No one offered to pick up her tab.

They didn't really know her,
the protesters explained.
When I left the bar the woman was outside
laughing with someone in a car
who had brought cash to pay her tab.
Inside the bar, everyone was happy.
When I left to go home
horse shit was still in the street.

Train Lady

JULIE ESTY

A dramatic monologue from the Dunmore Cemetery Tour

My name is Irene and I lived around here. I was born and raised here. Married and had children here in this valley. My two boys died when they were young, and the mines took my husband. It's hard losing your family. I had a lot of years of being lonely. I worked every day to make ends meet. I didn't make a lot of money. I just made ends meet. Sometimes, it was so hard figuring out how to pay the rent. Then something happened that made it even harder—the Stock Market Crash of 1929. The Great Depression hit. After that, nobody had any money. Those were tough, tough times. In 1931, I lost my job. At that point, I'd just had it. No family, no job, no money. I didn't know what to do, but I knew one thing—there was nothing holding me here. I thought maybe, just maybe, things could be better somewhere else.

So I gathered some of my things together, put on some of my husband's clothes that I'd kept, bundled up some food, and took all the money I had—$8.16 to be exact—and walked out of my house. Didn't even lock the door behind me—just left. I went downtown to the train station and got a train. I didn't buy a ticket either. In July 1931, I hopped a train. Yeah—I know what you're thinking. A woman—older—hopping a train. Well, I did it. Back then everyone was on the move looking for work. Riding the rails from town to town—crossing this country, looking for a miracle. A job—anything where they could make money to send home. It wasn't an easy life. Never knowing where you were going or going to get a meal from. Not knowing when work would come along or where you were going to sleep. I spent many hours in the camps—hobo camps. I wasn't lonely anymore, that's for sure. Always people in the train cars and camps on the move. Young men, old men, families, and even kids who should have been in school. The faceless thousands hit by the Great Depression. I was one of them. I shared many a meal of stale bread with a lot of people I didn't know. They were good people. Just fell on hard times.

I traveled for about four months with a teenage boy named Bobby. Met him in Ohio. He was looking for work so he could send money home to his ma. One day in Texas, we hopped a train. Hopping trains is a dangerous business. I'd gotten good at it. Bobby—he didn't make it that day in Texas. He missed and went under the wheels of the train. I missed Bobby and often thought of his ma waiting for him to come home one day and he never would. After Bobby, I mostly traveled alone. Spent fifteen months seeing this country, and I'll tell you—what a beautiful place it is. I saw the mountains and fields. Something about seeing the country looking out the door of a boxcar. Something about the clickety-clack of the train and watching the scenery go by. Kind of peaceful. We sure have a pretty country.

Like I said, I did that for almost a year and a half, and then I got tired. I missed the place I called home—the Lackawanna Valley. So I headed back. In October 1932, I hopped a train from New Jersey into Pennsylvania. You know, I'd seen so many wonderful sights in the past months but nothing as beautiful as Pennsylvania and the coal region. I rested my head back against the wall of the train car I was on. Thought I'd sleep for a bit. And that's where I passed on. Natural causes. Nothing like what happened to Bobby. It was just my time.

When the train pulled into Scranton, one of the railroad workers found me. He didn't know I was from this valley. I didn't take anything with me to identify me. Of course, the railroad employees called an undertaker, and I stayed in one of their establishments unclaimed for a few days. That was fine too. Then they found a nice, quiet resting place for me. Now my final rest is in the Home for the Friendless section of the Dunmore Cemetery in an unmarked grave. Doesn't bother me at all, because when all is said and done, I made it home. Home—to the beautiful Lackawanna Valley.

Little Miss Know-It-All

BARBARA J. TAYLOR

My Sunday-school-teacher, deaconess-in-church, member-of-the-PTA mother ran a World Series baseball pool out of her kitchen. I can't explain it. In the thirty-nine years I knew her on this earth, she never once showed an interest in sports, a trait I very much inherited.

Mom kept her pool simple. Ten players a day. Ten numbers, zero to nine. She'd write them out on torn strips of paper, fold them in half, and place them inside the only lidded cup we had, a chocolate milk shaker, free with the purchase of Hershey's Syrup. For a buck a chance, anybody could get in on the action. When the ballgame ended, she'd add up the scores from both teams. Whoever had the number on the end of that total won the ten-dollar pot.

All luck. No skill required.

In 1967, we moved into our house on Shawnee Avenue in Scranton. The following year, Mom started sending my sister Alice and me out walking our neighborhood to find players for her pool. I couldn't have been more than five that October, putting Alice just shy of nine. Our four-year difference made her "the boss of me" in spite of my protestations. Truth be told, I didn't have a leg to stand on. Still don't, all these decades later. Divine right goes to the elder sibling.

As such, my sister put herself in charge of the money envelope, but she let me carry the numbers. With one good whiff, I could catch the sweet scent of chocolate still clinging to the plastic cup.

"You do the talking," Alice would say when we approached a house.

"Wanna buy a chance in the pool?" I'd ask any person who answered the door.

"What pool?"

"World Series."

"How much?"

"A dollar."

At that point, we'd either get the brush-off or an invitation to step inside while our neighbor found his or her wallet. Once Alice collected the money, I'd pop off the lid, offer up the cup, and instruct, "Pick a number."

In 1968, the Tigers defeated the Cards in the final game of the World Series, 4–1, the only baseball score I ever committed to memory. It took the Tigers seven tries to win the title. That meant Alice and I went door-to-door seven times that first year.

Back then, we always stuck to our own neighborhood, a four-by-six near-rectangle of avenues and streets known as the Plot. Water defined its borders on three sides like a flat-bottomed U or a dropped stitch in the long scarf of river that cut Scranton in half on the diagonal. A set of parallel train tracks completed the perimeter.

Nana and Grampa Howells lived across those tracks, as did the boy who'd become my ninth-grade crush. For a solid year, I'd listen to the chugging heartbeat of a passing train and think, he can hear that too. Same engine. Same boxcars. Same steam-whistled warning on his side of the rails and mine.

Eventually, he'd give me my first "real" kiss under the Depot Street trestle, near where the pothole still opens up after a century of backfill and blacktop. Could be from groundwater, but I'm more inclined to blame the mines. That's how it is in old coal towns. Any minute, the earth might give way and cause a pothole, crack a foundation, or swallow you whole. Same goes for love. You could try playing it safe, but living is chance, and the thrill of a first kiss is a bet worth taking, even if he ends up breaking your heart.

Funny how one memory begets another. My mother's baseball pool. An adolescent crush. Two experiences, years apart, crossing paths on the other side of middle age.

In our younger days, Alice and I had a more linear approach to thinking. Take the pool, for instance. We had a routine. Start out at the Sweets' house and work our way down Shawnee Avenue. Athertons. Katulises. Sundays. Mr. Sunday's father lived one street over. The first time I saw him in the Plot, I stood wide-eyed, unable to speak. I knew him as the crossing guard up at Robert Morris Elementary, where he wore a black uniform and a peaked cap. He stopped traffic with a handheld sign before waving students to safety. Never did I imagine him in a cardigan and slippers with a home or a family or a life beyond his post. My failure to put two and two together embarrassed me. I liked being in the know.

Further up the block, we'd sometimes skip Mrs. Kipikash's house because she'd once yelled at my sister for carrying our new puppy instead of letting him walk. "You'll kill him if you drop him," she'd said. Not a minute later, he belly-flopped out of Alice's arms. Sure he was dead, she scooped him up and ran home sobbing. The pup came through unscathed, but my sister required a little time to lick her wounds.

We also scratched another house off the list because, according to Mom, the son was "bad news." She wasn't telling us anything we didn't know. The year his family moved in, he'd chased Alice and me around his cellar all jokey, except he was the only one laughing. We never went back there again.

I filed that memory away with other stuff I knew I wouldn't entirely understand until I got bigger. Like the contents of that paper bag Mom showed Alice when I was eight. They kept it hidden on a high shelf in the hall closet for something called their "time of the month." Or the punchline to the dirty joke Joan's older brother told when I was ten. It had to do with a little boy watching his naked parents from underneath a glass bed as if they couldn't see him or as if glass beds existed.

Joan's road ran perpendicular to Shawnee Avenue and dead-ended with a twenty-four-foot billboard on the bank of the Lackawanna River. I'll never forget the day the sky split in half, rain pouring on Joan's side of the street, sun shining on the other. For a good ten minutes, we darted back and forth, into the drops and out again, not another soul in sight to appreciate the miracle.

Her father died a few months later. At ten years old, I understood the meaning of those words, but I wouldn't feel their punch until my own dad passed away from old age.

Joan threw up at the funeral. I wasn't there to see it, but I remember hearing the story when I went over to her house for supper that night.

"You're Pearl's daughter," one of the relatives said to me from across the dining room table.

Knowing better than to talk with my mouth full, I nodded my response.

The woman nodded back, her hair bleached stiff like cornhusks. "So that makes you Maurice's granddaughter."

I shook my head "no" and swallowed. "I have a grampa named Carl and a grampa named Midge."

That should've been the end of it. A polite, "Sorry, I must be thinking of somebody else," whether she meant it or not. Instead, she poked harder. "What's Midge's Christian name?"

My cheeks burned with embarrassment. People called him Midge. I called him Grampa. "William," I finally said, relieved to have remembered. "Howells."

"He's not your *real* . . ." She chewed all the flavor out of that last word before taking her next bite. ". . . grandfather." As I struggled to make sense of the allegation, she added, "He's only your step-puh." Her bright red lips smacked together, giving the "p" its own syllable.

There were other adults at the table, but no one intervened. Maybe they were too exhausted or grief-stricken. Or maybe they were happy not to be in that woman's sights. *Children are resilient, and besides, she's not ours.*

My throat got sore the way it does when I hold back tears.

"Your mother's mother was married before."

That was a bald-faced lie. Mom would've told me for sure. Yet, just for a moment, the walls shifted, and I felt sick to my stomach, like you do when the car parked next to yours starts moving out of the blue.

"Her name is Caroline," the woman said.

The walls steadied. "No, it's not." Relief fueled my confidence. "My nana's name is Alice, like my sister."

The truth didn't stop her, though, and I suddenly wanted to go home, had to go home. After excusing myself, I marched out the door, down the block, and into my own kitchen where my parents and sister sat finishing their meal.

"Get a load of this," I said, launching my story with an expression I'd been dying to try since I'd heard it on television.

Somewhere between the cornhusk hair and the red lipstick, I noticed my family watching me, not listening-watching but watching-watching, like they felt sorry. I kept talking, so nobody else would, trying to get to the part about Caroline. If I could just get to Caroline, they'd see how crazy Joan's relative was.

All eyes dropped when I ran out of words.

Mom stacked the dirty plates, piled the silverware on top, and carried her load to the counter. On her trip back for the iced-tea glasses, she handed me a towel. "You can dry."

I knew enough not to argue, so I took my place next to her and stared at the steam coming off the water filling up the dishpan. "How can you stand it so hot?" I didn't care about the answer. I just wasn't ready to hear what she brought me over to say.

"You get used to it." She added a squirt of Joy to the water and swirled it into suds. "You will too when you're a housewife."

"No, I won't." I couldn't be sure if I was talking about washing dishes or being married. Either way, I decided to stick with my answer. I wanted something that came out of my mouth to be true.

Mom took a couple of long breaths. "That wasn't her story to tell," she said, her voice stretched tight.

My dad got up and adjusted the rabbit ears on the portable TV until *Dragnet* came in clear, but he kept the volume turned down to a whisper. Alice picked up a magazine and pretended to read.

I wanted to stew in my indignation, but curiosity got the better of me. "What story?"

"About Nana being married before." Mom turned the faucet down to a trickle for rinsing. "To my father."

"Grampa," I said, grabbing a dish from the drainboard.

"No." She leaned over the sink, opened the window, and pulled at her blouse. "A different man."

"Maurice?"

"Yes."

Another time, I would have caught my sister's eye to see her reaction to such a stunning revelation, but she already knew. They all knew, even Joan's family, and it made me feel lousy. "So what happened?"

"He never made a home for her."

I almost asked what she meant by that, but I didn't want to call any more attention to my ignorance.

"A few years later . . . " My mother's voice smoothed out. ". . . she met and married Midge."

Midge. Sometimes I'd hear her call him Dad, but mostly, it was Midge. *How did I miss that until now?*

"And just so we're clear." She looked at me like she was peering over a pair of reading glasses. "Midge *is* your grandfather. I don't care what that woman said."

I didn't care either. Not about the Grampa part. I loved that man. He was the one who called me "Little Buddy" and took me out "galivanting," his word for running errands. And when Alice and I stayed over, he'd pull the change from his pocket and give us a three-second peek. Closest guess won the money, but then he'd always find a little extra so no one went home empty-handed.

I adored Grampa. My upset had nothing to do with what I'd found out and everything to do with how. "Well," I said, grasping at my last chance for vindication, "Nana's name isn't Caroline." I'd have bet the house on that fact and won.

"You're right." Mom rinsed off the last of the silverware and emptied the dishpan.

"I *am* right. Where'd she come up with a name like that? It's not even close to Alice."

"Your guess is as good as mine."

I slid the pile of dry plates on the cupboard shelf and slammed the door. "Little Miss Know-It-All over at Joan's house doesn't know everything."

My mother gave me a look like she meant to scold me for name-calling. Instead, she said, "Little Miss Know-It-All has a lot to learn," and kissed the top of my head.

It would be years before I'd think to ask my sister how she'd found out about our grandmother's first marriage. "Nana and Grampa took me to Kmart one day." Alice screwed up her face like she was sucking on a lemon. "And I couldn't wait to ask them if they'd ever seen *Divorce Court* on TV."

I grinned. "Nana, of all people." My grandmother was the type of woman who took "prim and proper" as high praise. Ex-husband or not, she'd never be caught dead watching a show called *Divorce Court*. "What'd she say?"

"Not a word. You know Nana."

We all knew Nana. And loved her. But whenever one of us did something wrong, she'd give us the silent treatment. My mother took the opposite approach and became a yeller. Not mean. Just loud. When Alice was little, she used to tell her friends, "If my mom yells at you, it means she likes you." And my mother liked all the kids. She'd yell at us to stay off the riverbank. And to ride our bikes on the sidewalk. To stop screaming in the yard because it made her think one of us was hurt. To play nice. Take turns. Be kind.

"So what happened?" I asked.

"Mom told me. Not right away. I guess it took her a few days to get up the courage." Alice made a show of wiping her brow. "I thought I was in trouble when she finally sat me down."

In trouble. The worst place to be as a kid.

"Speaking of trouble," I said, "remember the time we bought ourselves hot fudge sundaes with the money Mom gave us to buy a birthday present?"

"*Her* birthday present," Alice said, and we laughed the way sisters do.

The seventh game of the 1968 World Series fell on October 10, the day before my mother's birthday. Thanks to Grampa, Alice and I had enough change between us to buy a chance in the baseball pool.

That morning, Mom had given us five dollars to buy her a birthday present.

Five dollars.

From her own pocket.

After school, Alice and I went to Burke's Drugstore in Green Ridge and bought their biggest bottle of Jean Naté body splash for the amazing low price of three dollars and fifty cents. A bottle that size would keep Mom smelling like fruit cocktail for years.

Proud of our thrift, we discussed how best to spend the remaining money. Go to the Handy Dandy, a five-and-dime across from Robert Morris, and buy Mom a second present, or head over to Epaul's Candy Shop for sundaes.

We inspected the Jean Naté, marveled at its heft, and agreed any other gift would pale in comparison.

Decision made, we skipped all the way to Epaul's for two scoops of vanilla ice cream each, hot fudge, whipped cream, and extra cherries. Sure, it was Mom's money, but she'd want us to treat ourselves.

Except she didn't.

We found that out as soon as we got home and told her about the ice cream.

"You did what?" The baseball game was playing on TV without the sound. Mom turned the set off anyway. That's when the yelling started.

About the money—it was hers. Thoughtfulness—a trait we lacked. Honesty—another attribute in short supply, though to be fair, we'd been completely honest about Epaul's. It's how we ended up in trouble in the first place. I opened my mouth to make that very point but reconsidered after Alice landed an elbow in my side.

"Two selfish girls," my mother said in a final burst of grievance. "Go out and play." She switched the television back on. "I'm tired of looking at you."

Mom didn't have to tell us twice. We hightailed it out the door and started griping as soon as we were out of earshot.

"Wait till she sees the size of the Jean Naté." Alice toed a rock out of the dirt and kicked it down the sidewalk. "Won't she be sorry."

I scoured the ground for my own rock. "Biggest bottle I ever saw."

Alice looked at me wide-eyed. "If she didn't want us to treat ourselves, she should've told us."

"Exactly." I found a rock-sized piece of coal and gave it a good kick.

"I thought mothers were supposed to be giving."

"Me too."

The conversation dropped off, and I found myself thinking about the previous night's supper. Dad took the extra pork chop, so Mom cut two nice pieces off hers for my sister and me.

Alice must have been having a similar thought because she threw her rock into someone's bushes and said, "She gives to us all the time."

"I know." The shame of our behavior took hold in my belly. "Bathroom!" I yelled and ran back to the house.

When I finished my business, Mom called me into the kitchen.

"I'm sorry," I said, tears welling.

"You won the baseball pool." She picked up the money envelope and poured its contents on the table, four singles and six dollars in change. "You and your sister are two lucky girls."

I stared at the pile of cash.

"Take it," she said. "It's yours, fair and square."

With the side of my hand, I swept the money into the envelope and pressed it against my chest.

"Two lucky girls," she said again. "Second chances don't come along every day."

I nodded vigorously.

"Now go tell your sister."

I raced out of the house and immediately spied Alice at the other end of Shawnee. "We won! We won! We won!" I yelled for two short blocks.

When I finally got close enough to tell her what we'd won, we took off for the Handy Dandy with our ten-dollar winnings in hand.

Our generosity knew no bounds. Dish towels, licorice, a deviled egg plate. Hot pads, Sen-Sen, Japanese perfume.

And after buying all that, we still had enough money left for the pair of ceramic dogs I'd been eying since we'd entered the store. They stood about four inches tall, but best of all, they were covered in a kind of glitter that magically changed color with the weather. Mom would never have to wonder if it was raining outside again.

And, of course, to top it all off, the world's biggest bottle of Jean Naté.

We wrapped as many presents as we could in the Sunday funnies and used regular newspaper on the rest. After dinner the next night, we piled the gifts in front of Mom, and she oohed and aahed over every single one. When she got to the Jean Naté, she said, "I'll never have to buy another bottle again," and laughed.

Dad surveyed the loot. "You made out like a bandit," he told her before taking everyone's picture.

"Who wants cake?" my mother asked, picking up a knife.

"We have to light the candles first. And sing." Alice fished a pack of matches out of the junk drawer.

"And you need to make a wish," I said.

"Already got my wish." Mom smiled.

"What's that?" Alice and I both asked at the same time.

"Two thoughtful daughters."

We agreed.

"And dogs that can tell the weather," I added.

"Can't forget those," Mom said, wiping glitter off the tablecloth and into a torn piece of newspaper.

Alice lit the candles three times that night so she and I could also take a turn at blowing them out.

Much to our disappointment, the Jean Naté only lasted about six months. The dogs hung on much longer, shedding glitter like snow inside Mom's shadow box. All these years later, it's the deviled egg plate that's become a family heirloom. I borrow it now and again, but when it's not in use, Alice keeps it in her china closet. Divine right endures.

As do some of the lessons I picked up childhood.

I may not know what possessed my mother to run a baseball pool, but because of her, I'm a firm believer in luck and second chances, even when they're undeserved. Especially when they're undeserved. And though, true to my word, I never got used to putting my hands in steaming hot water, I still think of love every time I hear a train pass by.

Enjoying a Smoke in Scranton

STEPHANIE LONGO

"It's a beautiful day," Dominic Keating began my first interview with him.

Two days earlier, on March 25, 2020, Governor Tom Wolf announced the initial stay-at-home order for several Pennsylvania counties. We were supposed to meet in downtown Scranton but switched to Zoom out of an abundance of caution. The day after, Pennsylvania confirmed its one thousandth case of COVID-19.

I'd been researching the story of Dom's family's business, Parodi Cigar Group, for a planned company history. When the pandemic ground archival research to a halt, Dom's oral histories—his voice—became my crucial basis for telling the story of this legendary Italian American brand. I didn't want to interview him digitally since I feared I would lose something in translation. We talked over Zoom, and despite the occasional "Can you still hear me?" or "I don't see you on my screen!" from his end, he made himself clear.

"The Suraci family are natives of Podargoni, a small mountain village in Calabria," Dom recounted. "In 1900, my great-grandfather worked there as a butcher. That year, my uncle Dominic was sixteen years old, and he decided to emigrate to New York. Our family didn't have much money, but my great-grandfather made sure his son could take English lessons as soon as he arrived in New York."

Young Dominic Suraci discovered that the burgeoning Italian American population in New York's Lower East Side had many small cigar makers manufacturing the Toscano cigar, which was, and still is, Italy's national cigar. When he realized that the cigar makers couldn't communicate with the tobacco farmers in Tennessee and Kentucky due to their lack of proficiency in English, Dominic decided to become the middleman by purchasing tobacco and having it delivered.

Dom's grandfather, Anthony, came to the United States in 1903 at fourteen, after Dominic told him how well things were going with the business he created.

"You know, this is a great country. I have a great business going. You'll work for me, and you'll do very well," Dominic said to his brother.

"Look, I've worked for Pop, and I didn't come over here to work for you. I'm going to find my own way," Anthony replied.

"You know what they say about the Calabrese, we have hard heads!" Dom laughed as he recounted the story. "My grandfather really resented it that his brother wanted him to work for him as an underling, but within about fourteen months, his pushcart was hit by a trolley. He would have been killed, except the trolleys going through the Lower East Side had a basket in the front to catch people before they fell under the wheels. He broke his leg, and his cart was destroyed. That's when Dominic paid him a fateful visit."

According to Dom, Dominic told Anthony, "It's too bad you got hurt. I know how much you want to go back to pushing that cart around, but you don't have any money coming in. Rolling cigars is something you can do while you're sitting down, and it will be something to provide you with some income."

In the years 1890 to 1910, before the mechanization of the cigar industry, people who made cigars by hand were among the highest-paid workers in the United States. A third Suraci brother, Francesco, came over in 1906 to join Dominic and Anthony in the family business.

"Just imagine, there were two brothers now on the pier to greet their youngest brother, and they said, 'Frank, now that you're here, you're going to work for both of us. We're going to set up our own cigar-making shop to go along with supplying tobacco. You're going to do very well.' Well . . . Frank's response was the same as Anthony's, 'I'm not going to be your underling,'" Dom recalled.

"Frank ended up going to work at a bituminous coal mine in Clarksburg, West Virginia," Dom continued. "He was slight in size, so when he arrived in Clarksburg, they made him a mule driver at the mine. According to Frank, if he were allowed to stay in the mines, he would have taken over the mine, and eventually, he would have become a mine owner and a wealthy man, except his mule kicked him in the forehead, and the mine owners put him on a train back to Jersey City.

"When Frank was well enough to understand his brothers, they said, 'We know how much you want to go back to that coal mine, but we're going to teach you how to do something that will bring you some income until you have regained your strength.' Frank became an excellent cigar maker, and that's how the Suraci brothers got into the cigar business."

Following World War I and stints in the United States Army for Anthony and Frank, the Suraci brothers realized that quotas passed in the Immigration Act of 1924 and subsequent restrictions on immigration from Italy might hurt their business.

"They came to feel that the only people smoking their cigars were Italians, and if there were no more young Italians coming to the US, then the market for their cigars would disappear . . . but here's where Scranton comes into the story," Dom said. "The brothers decided they were going to convert their factory in New York, which was a substantial operation, to making American-style cigars because there was no future in Italian cigars. In the meantime, they didn't want to lose the business they had with Suraci Brothers Italian cigars, so they found a manufacturer of Italian cigars in Scranton's West Side called Licata."

Italian-style cigars, like those made by the Suraci brothers, are made by what is called the Tuscan method, which involves air-curing the tobacco leaves, resulting in a lighter flavor and aroma. A popular method for producing American-style cigars is the "binder-wrapper" technique, where the binder and wrapper leaves are rolled together around the filler, creating a distinct flavor profile that is stronger than that of their Italian counterpart.

While the Suraci brothers' venture into American-style cigars didn't go as planned, their Italian-style cigars kept growing in popularity. In 1925, they were able to acquire the assets of the Parodi Cigar Company, including rights to the name. The brothers prospered, with Dominic living on an estate and Frank and Anthony living in upscale neighborhoods in Brooklyn.

"They had automobiles, and they were living the life," Dom explained. "But they made the mistake of going into the stock market at ten cents on the dollar margin buying. When the market crashed in 1929, they had to come up immediately with the losses that were associated with the big fall. On the day of the stock market crash, everything started as normal. Then the Parodi factory in Manhattan was hit. I'm going to tell you the story just how my Uncle Frank told me."

Dom lowered his voice as he solemnly repeated his uncle's words:

"Brother Dominic was in the office. I was doing the rounds in the plant, and Brother Anthony was out on sales calls. Shortly after lunch, I heard, 'Frank, come to the office, Frank, come to the office.' And I went in. Dominic, who was normally the most composed man, was with his head on the desk, and he was sobbing. He said, 'We've lost everything. We lost everything.' And Frank said, 'How could that be? Our sales are great. We're busy. What do you mean?' Dominic said, 'Our stocks. We had to cover the losses; we had to sell everything. There's nothing left.'

"They had to decide what to do," Dom added. "Dominic somehow didn't lose his house. The two younger brothers had fifty dollars each, I think, out of the petty cash that wasn't seized to cover the market losses. Dominic was to go back to selling tobacco to whatever little cigar makers still remained in New York, Philadelphia, or Boston, while Anthony and Frank would get to keep the Parodi Cigar name, even though the factory was gone.

"They remembered that Licata had been their subcontractor on making cigars, so they decided to come to Scranton to see if they could go to work for them," Dom continued. "The best thing the brothers had was their innovative minds, and they helped Licata a great deal, so much so that eighteen months after the Suraci brothers arrived in Scranton, they had reestablished enough credit that they were able to buy out Licata, and they resumed production of their Italian cigars.

"They took a national tragedy and turned it around, right here in Northeastern Pennsylvania," Dom said, tapping his finger on his desk for emphasis.

The successes continued for the Suraci brothers following their move to Scranton. In 1952, they bought out their largest competitor, De Nobili Cigar Co. of Long Island City, New York, and then in 1963, their next-largest competitor, Petri Cigar Company. In 1970, the company introduced its signature Avanti Cigar, flavored with an anisette tip. It went on to become the company's premier brand and one of their best-rated cigars. This style of cigar was so successful that the Parodi Cigar Group eventually reorganized as the Avanti Cigar Company, the name by which it is still known today.

I have nearly five hours of interviews with Dom, each minute revealing another layer of the Suraci family's story and how their lives and work weave into the historic landscape of both Northeastern Pennsylvanian and Italian American history, as we began to learn how to weave teleconferencing and other pandemic-related advances into our own daily lives.

And, to think, none of this would have been possible without three brothers from Calabria.

A Ted of Two Cities

TED LORUSSO

September—1978

I've moved to Manhattan from Scranton. I am determined to land a job in the film industry as the next Alfred Hitchcock. I knock on a hundred industry doors. No response. I knock on another hundred doors. Still no response. Money is running out. So I get a job as a waiter. That waiter job leads to another waiter job, then another, and another, until I land at Charlie's, a legendary Broadway hangout, a poor man's 21. To work at Charlie's is to mingle with theatrical luminaries and their assistants. Maybe I'll become the next David Merrick. Maybe I'll take up acting and become the next Uta Hagen. Maybe I'll write a play and become the next Arthur Miller.

I train for the requisite two days. My first shift is a Monday lunch, and my first customer has just sat. Confidence is high. I'd been waiting on tables for five years. I can handle this, even if it's one of the luminaries.

"Not to worry, Tiger," says Frankie D, a cowaiter, "Nobody important."

"How can you tell?"

"It's 11:30 in the morning. Nobody important comes in here before three in the afternoon. You'll be fine."

I grab ice water and a basket of bread and make for the table. It's all the way in the corner, exactly where I would sit if I was sitting here by myself.

My guy is in his sixties, tall, balding, thick glasses, long legs that jut into the aisle. He sports a clean white tee under a well-worn cardigan, jeans, and expensive old-man shoes. Rumpled but well-off. An air of dissatisfaction surrounds him. He's bent over the table reading a slim volume. He's not a theatrical luminary. Just a grumpy guy with a book. Must have wandered in by mistake.

"Good evening, sir," I say.

The guy looks at his watch, then at me. He has helpless, misty eyes. Or maybe he needs to clean his glasses. He cocks his head and looks down at his watch again. Ah, a perfectionist. "I mean, good morning, sir."

The guy nods, as if to say, "better."

"Would you like something to drink before din- . . . lunch?"

"Tea. Make sure it's hot," as he returns to his book.

"Yes, sir."

Most restaurants keep a pot of hot water on the back coffee burner for tea, but in my experience, it's never hot enough. This perfectionist wants his tea hot. So I'm gonna make it hot. I grab an individual metal teapot, drop in a teabag, fill it with the not-so-hot water, then walk it behind the line and put it directly under the broiler. On a tray I place a cup, saucer, spoon, lemon wedge, and a couple of creamers. I wait exactly one minute. Then, using two napkins, I carefully secure the screaming hot teapot on the tray, and head for his table.

"Here you go, sir," I say, setting the teapot, cup, and saucer in front of him. "Use your napkin to pour. It's damn hot."

The guy squints, his eyebrows meet above his nose; it's clear he's never heard a waiter say "damn." He grabs the teapot with naked fingers, quickly whips his hand back.

"Told you," I say, emboldened by the fact that he's too old to hit me.

"That you did. What's the soup today?"

"We have two. Split pea and chicken noodle."

"How's the pea soup?"

"Coagulated. You could hang wallpaper with it."

It's an old waiter's trick. Warn a customer off a certain item—even though it's probably perfectly OK—because it makes him feel as if he's being well looked after, as if he's in on the secret.

"How's the chicken noodle?"

"Fresh this morning."

It wasn't, but he'll never know.

"I'll take it."

"Bowl or cup?"

"Bowl. Extra crackers. Lots of noodles."

Serving soup is easy. Grab a bowl. Underline it with a plate. Ladle the soup. Line the under-liner with crackers. I do so, making sure to get lots of guts—that is, noodles. I walk the soup to the table. The guy has his fingers in the ice water. I set the soup in front of him and wait, like Jeeves. The guy nods and, with his free hand digs, in. I return the nod and walk away.

Minerva, floor manager and nonapologetic star-fucker, arrives even later than usual. Removing his coat, he scans the dining room. When he sees my guy, his eyes pop. He hightails it to Frankie D.

"Who has table 101?"

"The new guy," says Frankie D.

"The new guy? Are you nuts?"

Minerva trundles over to me and quivers. His real name is Mervin. Chubby, forty, dressed like the oldest member in a glee club, he's an actor-singer-dancer who never acted, sang, or danced in any show, anywhere. I learn later that they call him Minerva after "Mrs. Miniver" because he acts like a crusty old woman living through a war.

"I'll bring the check to 101," Minerva squawks, "got it?"

"I'm sorry, what—?"

"When table 101 is ready for his check, I'll bring it. I'm not kidding. Don't fuck with me on this."

"OK," I say and back up, not from fear but because Minerva's breath smells like an open grave.

Frankie D gets a party of four businessfolks and snaps to it. All I have is my single. Nothing to do but wait discreetly and keep an eye on Minerva keeping an eye on my one table. Twenty minutes later, the guy finishes his soup, sits back, and sticks his fingers back in the ice water. I casually approach the table.

"More tea?" I ask.

"No!" the guy says, practically shouting in alarm.

"Something else? Burger. Tuna sandwich?"

"No. Soup was enough," he says.

I'm feeling sympathetic, so I ask, "What are you reading?"

"Garbage," he says, and holds up a battered copy of *Death of a Salesman*.

"Oh, that. I never saw it."

"Indeed . . . you and the other half of the globe."

"I'm sorry?"

"China is about to get an earful. Check. Please."

I find Frankie D and ask for help, as it's my first ever check for Charlie's. Together we add the soup to the tea . . . tack on New York state sales tax . . . staple calculator slip to check. I slip it inside a plastic check-presenting tray and call Minerva over.

"101 wants his check."

Minerva smooths all three of his hairs and grabs the check. He walks to table 101 as if he's in a royal procession. I watch him place the check on the table; watch him back up two paces; watch him genuflect.

Minerva spews incoherently. My guy says, "Thanks," and hands Minerva an American Express card. Minerva takes the card and sprints it back to me. I run it. Minerva grabs it and is off. He places the check on my guy's table like he's presenting a baby to King Solomon. My guy signs the check, looking up with ill-disguised disgust. Minerva genuflects once more, then scoots off.

My guy rises and gathers his coat. I help him with it.

I say, "So did the host just genuflect before you?"

"That he did," he says with finality.

"Sorry about that. He probably mistook you for a saint."

"I get that a lot," he says and holds out his hand. "Don't worry, I'll be back. What's your name?"

I take his hand; it's firm like a catcher's mitt. "I'm Ted. Ask for me next time. I'll keep the supplicants at bay."

"I will, Ted," he says. He turns to go but stops, turns back, like there was something he missed. He says, "Most of these guys here don't want to be here. They want to act. Sing. I guess dance. What about you?"

His query takes me by surprise. When taken by surprise, I often sound like a duck-billed platypus singing the national anthem. I manage to spit out, "I'm thinking about writing a play . . . maybe?"

He lowers his head and leans in. "Heat up a pair of knitting needles and jam them into your eyes," he says, "It'll have the same effect." Then he pokes me in the chest and walks out.

Minerva's in my face again, spewing cadaverous halitosis.

"What did he say to you? What did he say to you?"

"He wanted to know my name."

"Did you tell him?"

"Of course."

"He didn't ask me for my name."

"When he comes in again, I'll introduce you."

"Don't you—How dare you? Do you know who that was?"

"Just some rumpled guy with a book," I say.

"That was Arthur Miller. You just waited on Arthur Miller, the greatest playwright ever, living and/or dead."

I look at the signed Amex slip. "Your Mr. Miller is a lousy tipper." Minerva snatches the check and huffs off. Frankie D calls to me as he passes by with an armload of burgers.

"You got Joey Heatherton and friends on 303."

"The Joey Heatherton? I thought you said no one important comes in before three."

"Tell that to Joey."

September—2013

I can no longer afford my apartment, so after thirty-five years in Manhattan, I move back to Scranton. Two months in, my NYC unemployment runs out and I need a job. I have one marketable skill: waiting on tables. I get a job at a family-owned Italian restaurant two blocks from where I'm staying. It's a three-star restaurant in this two-star town. It's owned and managed by Debbie. I look forward to showing her—and Scranton—what I know about the restaurant business.

My first day of training, I meet Dawn: thin, wiry, intense. She's headwaiter and the person who will train me.

This is going to be so damned easy—I say unto myself—a breeze.

And Dawn says: "This is Debbie's restaurant. Her name is on the sign; her name is on your check. We do things her way, otherwise she gets mad. And you do not want to get her mad."

Who is this woman who reeks of garlic and Jean Naté?

"Are you talking to yourself?"

"I think so."

"Well, keep it down. You'll disturb the customers." She goes on, "Never go behind the bar during service, or Debbie'll get mad. Pick up your drinks the moment they're ready, or Debbie'll get mad. Get water and a basket of bread to your tables one minute after they sit, or Debbie'll get mad. Don't mistake the white for the red clam sauce, or Debbie'll get mad. We have a ton of doctors and lawyers, politicians and judges, and one priest who packs a .38-caliber special. You have to know how to handle him, otherwise you might get shot, and Debbie'll get mad."

Honey, I say unto myself,
I can handle a priest with a pistol
I've waited on Kings and Queens
Kennedys and Kramdens
Presidents and Pedophiles
I've waited on every religion known to science
Catholics and Jews
Muslims and Hindus
Satanists and sex addicts
Lutherans even
I snorted coke table-side with Joey Heatherton
I wrestled Andrew Cuomo for a dinner roll

I spilled red wine on Lady Sarah Churchill's white frock . . . and survived
I've worked weddings
Christenings
Bar Mitzvahs
Birthdays
Funerals
First dates
Last dates
Break-ups
Engagements
Divorces
Sweet Sixteen
I even catered Brises
I was the Bris king of Midtown Manhattan
Temple Chesed made me an honorary mohel
I can circumcise people, for Chrissake
I know what I'm doing

"Is it true that you used to wait on tables in Manhattan?" Dawn asks at last. "I wouldn't talk too much about it, though. This is Scranton. You'll sound all know-it-all, and Debbie'll get mad."

The Five Seasons of Scranton

THOMAS KIELTY BLOMAIN

I

When it snowed they closed the roads
Crossing the big hill of Delaware Street
And kids from all around came with sleds
To trudge up and fly down using wax paper
On the runners to go even faster
Again and again until you were numb
Before going home wet and cold and tired
With something frozen into your soul
That bound you forever to this place

II

Then came the many Masses of May
Attending church every day at Saint Paul's
With the kneeling and standing
The sitting and fidgeting
Until a nun hauled off and cracked you from behind
Not even nine years old and forced
To invent sins to confess in the dark chapel
Polluted with incense
But outside the blinding sun and honest air
Actually proved something true
Of that God they bragged about around here

III

In the heat we splashed in the dirty stream
That ran by the steaming blacktop playground
Behind Longfellow School where girls hopscotched
And wove lanyards from plastic strands while we climbed
The high chain-link fence with the sharp barbs at the top
Intended to protect us by threat of injury
From the mischief of getting away

IV

When the cool weather came
The sweet musk of anthracite corruption
Brought a touch of mystery to the air
All through the Green Ridge neighborhood
Where we played flashlight tag at dusk
Digging to hide in leaf piles higher than our heads
Before going home to baths and bed
Dirty like the old miners in our famous stories
And full of a bit of their same sad glory

V

Still a kid facing the mine cave of old age
Cast amid the love-hate relationships of this place
I continue to give myself guided tours of my past
Pointing things out to no one else aloud
As I walk through Nay Aug Park
Not far from where I live each day
Noting sixty years of change and decay
Both in myself and in this strange haven
Sensing a troubling shift in the coming darkness
And yet at least I know that whatever happens
From this point forward I had the good fortune
To grow up when I did

In the bewildered bloodline of Scranton
And I can keep laughing inside as I always have
Oddly self-satisfied at all the rest of it

Phylum Familia Immigrandorum

ANDREA TALARICO

In Memoriam John Kuckirka and Helen Talarico

*"The majority of plants that grow in vacant lots and along roads are aliens.
Hundreds of wayside plants came from Europe. The list is long: Black Mustard,
Red Clover, Wild Carrot and many, many others . . . the first known station for
a foreign plant is often at a seaport or along a railroad track."**

My mother's father comes from a place
that no longer exists on the map.
Erased. Nameless.

I traveled with him to a great green field,
a space in southern Poland where the
Carpathians created a soft
fold of arms, a valley of tall grass
and wildflowers spotted with small squares
of stone, foundations of houses long since
burned down or rotted out from within.

We all saw the armed guards spotting the
distant tree line, far enough away
and green enough to look like child's toys,
and none of us mentioned them, not one,
nor the country on the other side
of their rifle-made boundary.

"This is how you know it was once
a real place," our cousin translated,
gesturing at sweeps of cement left

crumbling from former sewage systems,
from village wellspring and water,
"That they shared resources,
that roots were planted."

My eyes sought the single solid
structure of a church, cresting the hill
to our north, its white steeple pointed
up at the bright August sun, haloed,

and I watched his face as he took
it in, my grandfather, gone somewhere,
perhaps, like me, watching a silent
film of his grandparents, praying their
way up and down a mountain each
Sunday to praise the god of this vale.

We are told that this is where
they practiced faith, the *Lemko* people,
a word that means *only*, a word that makes
me think, *singular*, makes me think,
all that's left.

Gazing across that hollow, in my
mind I build the frames of the homes that
my grandfather memorized the names of:

Warholic, Kucirka, Smerechna.

From the side of the dirt road, I will
pick a stem of Queen Anne's lace, press it
between the pages of my journal,
stow it home across the Atlantic.
When customs asks me if I am
importing any non-native flora,
I look to my grandfather. We call him Pa.
I say no, and know I say it for protection.

*"These immigrants almost invariably grow in disturbed soils, few of them venture far from the roadside, where they apparently cannot compete with our preadapted native flowers. Conversely, most native flowers cannot compete along the roadside."**

My father's mother comes, too, from a place
erased. Taken out of existence.

If you ask her, she will tell you
she is American, the only
one of her siblings not born in
Lebanon, she wouldn't remember
the long sail across the Atlantic
made without their patriarch, Domit,

Exiled years earlier, now living
in Brazil, amongst Jesuits, where
he studied alchemy's secrets
alongside his Catholic brethren.
He would later reunite with his
family in America, and
the story of the legalities

gets lost in the veined history of
how hard it must have been, a man's life
without a country, a home, his wife,
children, work; no place to lay roots down,
their village, Berkzala, erased,
no longer named on the maps of the world.

*"Can seeds remain viable in the soil for half a century or more, until succession renders their habitat suitable again?"**

When I tell my grandmother the name of
my new Brooklyn neighborhood, her face
lights up with memory, a key inserted
into a disused music box, woke.

She remembered special trips to the
city, tasked to trek with sister Mary
to Atlantic Avenue in
Brooklyn, to bring back with them grape leaves,
sumac, albums in Arabic, both
to hear and taste history but maybe too
to see themselves reflected in the world.

It's been half a century and I
live so close to where she endeavored
to find some home to bring home, I walk
the streets and spot the vestiges of
community in diaspora,
veins on a leaf:

Sahadi's, Damascus, Merhib.

*"It's concerning when a non-native plant immediately thrives. Experts are
still grappling with the question of whether an imperiled species can also be a
menace."**

What is the name for a plant that is
no longer considered native to
any place?

What is the name of a
homeland once war uproots it out
of existence?

What is immigration if not an
evolution, a turning toward
the sun, like leaves do?

I am Smerechna, Berkzala,
am Sicily, too, Calabria,
Denbighshire, color-blended and diverse,
sturdy as a Persian stonecress, blooming
pink alongside a busy highway,

reaching my face up through the wind and
rushing cars and ocean of noise to
receive God.

*Sources:

Roger Tory Peterson and Margaret McKenny, *A Field Guide to Wildflowers: Northeastern/Northcentral North America* (Boston: Houghton Mifflin Company, 1968).

Marion Renault, "The Waterwheel in Crisis," *New York Times*, August 13, 2019 (D1, D6).

Three Poems by Gerard Grealish

A View of Scranton

From the Hill
                Southside at dusk. Houses
with the merest spaces between them seem joined
to house the quiet outside. Stones
in cemeteries seem a continuum of stone;
there are certain mausoleums
not unlike steeples and mosques scattered here.

Here there is a power the builders could not divine
as if the place itself conspired a finishing touch.
The clatter of forks and knives goes unheard
and to the west the sky that is orange
darkens.

Monologue at Scranton's Historic Ironworks

Where men sweated and heat
smelted iron
                    icicles
hang from stone; pigeons
flap against cylindrical walls
leave droppings
on the stone floor.

Hard to tear down
this brick upon brick
built thick as prison walls
and no need to. Nothing
wants to be here. Out of sight
the city prospers
cut from the same rock ridge.

Here a shouting voice
grows further away
as if it spoke in another time.

The Step Falls
(adjacent to Nay Aug Park)

There is a desire to dive into this wall
of water
        drench our bodies in the rush of white and plunge
into the pool below.

It is not a sane desire. Though it is cool there
and here the heat wears away at us
                              steps
of stone brick are bedrock to the falls.

Thirty feet across and forty down it is a power
we would be taken by. After months
waiting to bare our bodies to the sun we wait now
for the tingling movement of the falls.
We see the vague outlines of stone
that seem the design of water.

The Indian American Dream

JANVI PATEL

I am an Indian American and somewhat of a disappointment to the family. Not because I have an American-like zero-spice tolerance but because I am currently majoring in English. *I hear the gasp.* Immigrant families leave their homes for bigger opportunities, setting aside individual desires for the collective gain. My family did that when they came from India to Scranton, determined to live their dreams through their children. That's where they stumbled. Their sacrifice for me assumed my sacrifice for them. It meant preparing and pursuing the careers they wanted but left behind. I thought we were to run after our dreams in this new country and go some extra miles if we had to. *They did.*

I've already sacrificed, though. As the child of immigrants, I had a job from my earliest years. It included being a translator from time to time, defending my parents against racism, making sure to use my American accent, doing well in school to prove my future success with report cards, and also being mindful of finances without letting the parents know. *The rule was: never tell your immigrant parents what fruit you like because the next day, you'd have a Himalayan mountain worth of it to eat.* You have a job that you do (out of concern) *for* your parents who work hard for *your* future. An immigrant child's success story is supposed to start with her parents climbing the community's social standing through her success. I was supposed to be a doctor, engineer, or lawyer because that's what success meant to my parents and to the people who looked at us as unwelcome outsiders. *Let's just say I became an English major to fight the racists.*

My mother, aka Mummy, was a pharmacist. That is, before she came to America, where her education was worthless. *I'd be pissed, to say the least.* Yes, my mother could have put herself through college again, but there was a slight problem. *English.* Not only would my mother have to learn EVERYTHING from scratch, but she would also have to learn a new language as an adult. Imagine being the smartest of your siblings and then feeling dumb just because you're in a different place. I remember the day I took my mother to a drive-through at McDonald's. She had never been to one, so it was like seeing a child at Disney. It seemed like magic when the operator asked what you wanted through the machine and then we picked it up at the window without stepping a foot outside our car. Now that I think of it, that was me introducing my mother to the America that I understand. How would she have known? She has spent her American life as an immigrant working at Aramark in a labor job.

My parents immigrated from India at a good time for the Electric City, the early 2000s. *It was when Scranton had consistent weather and the economy was booming.* We would spend many of our weekends just shopping through the crowd at Steamtown Mall. *Well, my mother would shop, and I would get bribed with ice cream.* I don't remember what the shop was called, but I remember how kind the lady who worked there was. Sadly, one of the first shops to close was that ice cream place. That was the only place I liked getting the cotton candy flavor from. *I never got it again.* I'd get frustrated when we'd have to make the long walk to our car after all that shopping. *Now there's always a place to park.* There was a fountain centered on the first floor, where people would toss in coins to make a wish. *I never wished for anything; I was just happy about being able to toss the coin.* Strangely, it's the only time when you're angry about having dollar bills instead of coins.

I used to be self-conscious at the mall because people were often quite openly racist. It was nearly a crime to be Brown and in the clearance section, where they assumed I was casing the place if not actively shoplifting. *Do you have any idea how many businesses, hotels, and motels we Gujaratis own, ma'am? Keep walking.* Not to mention some of the neighbors that hated when my mother cooked food that set the fire detector off. It was clearly not Indian-family friendly and still isn't designed for us. Now, we've moved out from the apartment to a house, the landmark of an immigrant's success.

Racism was a nightmare that I recognized but couldn't name. I didn't know the word. I only knew that my second-grade teacher treated me differently but didn't know there was a word with a long history to answer "why." She accused me of cheating off a student that sat across from me. *We had two folders in front of us like a wall. How could I have cheated?* Today, I would immediately report that. However, I spent my entire second grade under stress. One night, I even wet the bed. The next day, I was still confronting racism. The teacher usually assigned someone to hold the American flag to say the Pledge of Allegiance. I would recite it in my mind instead of saying it out loud. She thought I would get embarrassed if she asked me to do it and I couldn't, so she called on me. I walked up to her without making eye contact, held the flag, and recited the pledge flawlessly. When I finished, I handed the flag back and calmly walked to my seat without looking at her. From the corner of my eye, I could see the frustration on her face. Despite her targeting me, I couldn't disrespect her or talk back to her. My grandparents had taught me how Hindus view their educator as god in human form. Besides, as I refused to push back at her, she got more and more frustrated. She wanted a reaction from me that she could punish. I never gave her one. I like to think that will always color the way she thinks about Indian children.

Sometimes I can be an ambassador. When I shared pictures of my cousin's wedding with my teacher at Scranton High School, she was amazed. *I may have convinced my divorced and middle-aged high school science teacher to get married again.* Clearly, I had gotten more comfortable with my background by high school, and I had worked hard for it. When I went to India for my cousin's wedding, I bought shawls as gifts for my teachers. When I was shopping for them, the lights went out in the tiny shop. The lights go out sometimes, but they have great customer service in India. When you go into clothing shops, the staff actively shows you clothes by taking them out from the packaging. If you shop for shoes, they have a big square open in the ceiling from where the shopkeeper can shout foot sizes and the man up there will throw it down. I missed Christmas in America that year, but I found the same childlike joy in India. I wanted to bring my teachers the best souvenirs from India, and I did. When I went to hand my creative writing teacher the shawl, another teacher was there in the hallway. While my teacher admired the shawl, the other asked if I made it. *As if that's all we're made to do or can do.* I softly said no and stopped at that. My teacher refused to look at her colleague and calmly followed, "But she chose it, and I love it," and asked if she could give me a hug. As I turned after the hug, I saw her draping the shawl around her neck, as though she were proud of my background with me. So when the principal called on the eighth Patel of the row on my graduation day, I stood up with pride. Spoiler: I wasn't the last one. *We had only finished calling the female Patels.*

Geographically, physically, I am away from my roots. I never had an opportunity to bond with my culture as those who are born in India get to do. We visit often as a family, and I have seen much of the culture up close. But even there, I'm different, at least partly American, and I have to represent cultures that are oceans apart. *Don't ask me how many. My geography is weak.* This is exactly why my brown eyes twinkle in red and green during Christmas. I enjoy seeing those around me happy even if I'm not fully part of it. As much as I love a snowy Christmas, my heart still craves those nine nights of Garba where I can enjoy doing Dandiya Raas.

Recently, from the curiosity I possess as an English major, I decided to learn more about what Garba represents and symbolizes. I learned that Garba comes from the Sanskrit word *garbha*, which means "womb." It is performed in a circle, which represents the Hindu cyclical view of time. The picture of Goddess Durga is placed in the center, around which we dance barefoot, connecting to the goddess, as well as Mother Earth. The goddess at the center remains an unchanging constant force. Garba worships and celebrates the feminine form of divinity, Durga, who is known for her nine forms. I'm not close enough to think I already know enough, so I ask questions and learn.

I'm not alone in that twoness, though. We have a real expatriate community here. The Indian "uncle" at the Indian store in Scranton sold DVDs of newly released Indian movies. I never knew the store's actual name or even if it identifies as an Indian store anyway. But it felt like a place we belonged. There are currently three stores I know as Indian stores because they sell solely Indian products and food. They sell the same things: Thums Up, Kurkure, Parle-G, and other grocery items, but that's never made them compete with each other. In fact, when they run out of things, they recommend going to the other's place. *Here, we address each other as if we were relatives: uncle, sister (*ben*), brother (*bhai*), child (*beta*), grandpa (*dada*), grandma (*ba*). That's why so many women have "ben" behind their names or why we automatically add "ben" to another Indian friend's name. That's also why I addressed the storekeeper as uncle.*

I have lived in Scranton all my life, yet I am a complete Indian by heart. *My heart practically beats in Hindi, with Karan Johar directing every romantic scene.* I am an English major, but English was not my primary language. It is only my *greatest pride*. It's my journey from having started as an English Second Language student at John Adams Elementary School to taking English honors and AP English classes at Scranton High. I had to work to become someone who could even conceivably major in English. Except I forgot that my achievements had a racial background and that being good at English had nothing to do with being an Asian child. *Racism did a backflip.* I'm here to set it right. I'm an Indian American woman writer with lots to say. LOTS! Although this feeling of twoness resides in me, it continues to drive my love for knowledge. I realize I have more than my parents ever had or will have. I have TWO of EVERYTHING! Two celebrations, two languages, two identities, and two communities I can call mine. And as I descend from my room into the kitchen, I know India is somewhere near me, waiting for me to rediscover it in my own way. I am here in NEPA, yet it's so close; I can smell it! The smoke detector goes off, and I rush to grab a hand towel. It's never a fire. Just something my Indian mom cooked in the Scranton home we share.

Reclamation

PAULINE PALKO

My mother watched JFK's assassination while holding my bottle and poured all of her fear into that tepid potion. Like Charlie Brown, by the time I was nine, I had developed pantophobia. Charlie at least had Lucy's guidance for the price of a cold, hard nickel; I had to figure things out for myself.

Cheerleading and ballet looked fun, but I spent four years on the sidelines, safe from embarrassing stares, yelling the cheers along with the crowd. No cute little skirt for me. I wanted to try singing on the stage, but when the tryouts were posted for the spring musical, I signed up for a chorus part, where a missed note would go unnoticed. I dreamed of flying airplanes, interviewing celebrities, riding camels, and painting portraits that hung in museums. My mother insisted that joining the air force would get me raped and lead me into drugs and that college was not for me. Be a hairdresser, she advised. You don't need an education to get married and have kids. The things I wanted to do and couldn't stacked up, but I didn't follow her plan either. I worked mindless jobs during the day and, at night, sustained my dreams with words on pages.

When she died, I screamed like hell and started living.

The House in the Hills

LIZZY KE POLISHAN

One day in the early summer, on my husband Jason's off day, we decided to go out to Cooper's seafood restaurant for lunch. Jason loves seafood more than anyone I know. He grew up near the ocean, in Fujian, where he ate buckets of the freshest seafood—mussels, clams, crabs—nearly every day of his life, for super cheap. Here, in Scranton, a landlocked city in a landlocked state, seafood is much more expensive and nowhere as fresh. But we still go to every seafood and sushi restaurant in Scranton, just to try.

The GPS brought us through the Hill Section, on a street near my childhood home. On an impulse, I made a detour to show Jason the big white house where I lived until I was six, with my whole maternal family— my mom, grandparents, three uncles, and one aunt. I couldn't show Jason the inside, with its five stories and secret passageways and endless bookshelves built right into the walls, and with the creaky elevator that sometimes trapped its rider inside for hours until the elevator man could free them—but at least he could see the outside of this house, the setting of so many of my childhood stories.

I could imagine the house with no effort.

Outside, there was an enormous oak tree and an uneven sidewalk where I drew chalk hospitals for injured insects. My mom and I walked up and down the street to collect flowers and leaves that we pressed between pages of enormous books. The house had slate stairs flanked by ornate white planters that my grandma filled with red geraniums in summer and with sunburst-orange marigolds in fall.

The house had an amazing covered porch, painted the blue-gray color of the sky on a stormy day, that stretched across the front of the house. The right half was enclosed in glass, and the left half was round, bounded with pillars and a bunch of huge hydrangea bushes. I loved to go in the earthen hallway between the hydrangeas and the porch to play or read books. In the summertime, with the mosquito candles lit, my aunts and uncles and their friends sat outside listening to music, drinking beer, and enjoying my grandma's cooking. (Sometimes I tried to serve my specialty, Water Soup, which was exactly as awful as it sounds—lukewarm water with unpeeled vegetables and surprises, including cinnamon, black pepper, and rocks.) In October, we transformed the porch for Halloween. We stretched globs of fake spiderwebs between the pillars and set up animatronic witches and skeletons to greet guests. Every year, the decorations got more extravagant, and as a kid I was terrified of—but also in love with—the holiday, which also included a party where my grandma served huge amounts of buffalo chicken dip, wimpies, and festive desserts like witchy cupcakes or a strawberry Jell-O molded brain.

———————

I parked behind the stop sign in front of the house, in the shadow of the old oak tree.

The house looked totally different. The paint was peeling off in strips, hanging like worn-out Band-Aids off a leg. The porch looked—naked? It took me a second to realize that all the hydrangea bushes had been chopped, revealing the foundation, which was shabby and starting to rot. Through the front window, I could see a living room—but not my living room. There was unfamiliar furniture in a room painted a strange color—a room that looked nothing like the room I remembered, with its enormous boxy TV and the squashy black couches where my grandpa relaxed with a glass of scotch.

In the passenger's seat, Jason looked up and down the street.

"What's this?" he said, confused. I realized that since the house had no significance to him, he had no way of knowing that the house itself was what we had stopped to see. He probably thought we were lost.

I wanted to tell him that this was the house that I grew up in. The site of all those happy childhood memories, the place I always talked about with so much love.

But . . . it wasn't?

I felt so weird. Was it that place? Was it really?

Had it always been like this, run-down and imperfect, and I just hadn't noticed?

Or did the place where I grew up no longer exist? Maybe it wasn't just that I couldn't go inside but that I couldn't go back there at all.

I told Jason that this was my childhood home, though I felt strange saying the words.

"Oh," Jason said. "Old!"

He was right—it was old and falling apart—but I was annoyed. Not at Jason, but at the house itself. It *was* old. It wasn't what it was supposed to be. It wasn't what it had been. What I still wanted it to be. How was I supposed to show Jason something that wasn't there?

When everyone moved out of the big house, it felt like my family was coming apart. Like we were a dandelion that got blown into the wind. I wanted to be a planted dandelion again, round and whole, everyone attached to that one central stem.

The thing that I actually wanted to show Jason wasn't the building, wasn't the physical structure. The house itself had its charms, but it wasn't *the thing*.

The thing I wanted to show Jason—the thing I actually cared about—was the experience of everyone gathering and being gathered. All those everyday moments of being together.

And, as I reflect on it, those moments still happen, though now they take different forms.

It is standing around the island in the kitchen at my mom's house, with my mom and stepdad and my brothers and Jason; we pack sticky rice laced with nuts and minced pork into soaked banana leaves that we roll into fragrant cones for the Dragon Boat Festival. It is Easter dinner at my grandma's house, where everyone gathers to eat *hrudka* and *halupkis* and ham, and a cake in the shape of a lamb, and to have "Egg Wars," where we smash dyed eggs into each other head-on until only one uncracked winner remains. It is hosting dinner, at Jason's and my house, inviting my uncle Tim and his wife and four kids over to share fried rice and barbecued squid, and egg custards topped with abalone and baby scallops and goji berries. It is in my mom's garden, planting flowers during the pandemic. It is at my Aunt Tiffany's house, for Jason's and my wedding reception, where everyone shared a pot of incredible seafood soup that my Aunt Tiffany made from scratch, and everyone in my family came together to make something so beautiful in under ten days.

These moments no longer happen at that particular house, and they never will again. But they are still happening. They never stopped happening. And Jason has experienced them, has become a part of them. I don't have to show Jason the house. He already knows what I mean.

My childhood house is gone, but the experience of the "house" exists, with expanded boundaries—the "house" is still here, scattered across several houses, across the city, across time.

The moments lost their house-sized shape, but they have expanded to include Jason and new aunts and uncles and stepfamily and cousins and siblings. They didn't decay with the house. They got bigger—dandelion seeds, and all the space between them.

Three Poems by David Elliott

These Words

The way these words
make the day
go faster
speeding through dull scenery
on forgotten roads
punctuated by fence posts
and billboards
cows disappearing behind barns
with signs for chewing tobacco
too fast to read
and the road goes on
straight into night
radio stations wandering
onto the dial from distant states
playing a few country tunes
before fading
then through the static
a voice talking in a monotone
almost a form of static itself
talking about poetry
and just when it begins to matter
another station
elbows its way into the air
with a string quartet
one of Bartok's last
passionate
complex and dry
sawing through the night
and suddenly you're there
a destination inevitable and
puzzling because you've forgotten
wherever it was you wanted to go

but the door looks so inviting
your key fits
and there are
all these children
greeting you home after another day.

Ladybugs

everywhere—
tapping at the window, traversing
the computer screen, scaling
the earphone cord that dangles
next to the computer, gathering
and mingling between the back
door and the storm door,
crossing the place mat past my bowl
of oatmeal, and one flying
ungainly into the light
of a late autumn afternoon,
leaving my unkindled house,
frantic for home.

After the Party
for Carolyn

In a room full of plants
you've made strong

you make the crystal bowl
ring before shutting it away.

No voices, no cars,
a scattering of snow—

stillness after
a night of rooms filled

with talk, friends
and strangers face to face.

You ping it again,
bell of dawn swelling

and fading at once.
You are that sound

a clear ringing, round and open
as you pace the house.

Scranton the City, Scranton Myself

MAUREEN MCGUIGAN

Through the rusted bars in front of the arches, I see the Giant's Thrones. That's what I called the remnants of hardened moss-covered iron when I was little. The Scranton Iron Furnaces, built in 1840, were a massive facility in South Side near Roaring Brook that once made T-rails for the railroad during the Civil War. Coal would become king, but Scranton formed out of iron.

I have been here since 7:00 a.m., setting up for Bonfire at the Iron Furnaces, a fall cultural festival I cofounded as a celebration of immigrants—some originally from Western Europe but now from Central and South America, Africa, and Asia. Along with other dedicated volunteers, I tie cornstalks to tent poles, arrange pumpkins, haul hay bales, and carry tables. One nicks my leg so blood flows down my shin. I take a break and stare through this arch into the city's past, trying to see its future.

In college, I thought I would be translating German Dadaist poetry in Berlin. But my destiny was shaped by choices unnoticed. I didn't plan to come home after graduate school in 2002. I didn't have a plan at all. But home is where you go when you don't know what to do next.

I grew up in Scranton in the late seventies and eighties, when it was the poster child for "deindustrialization," a word I would not learn until later. A word conjuring rust and decay. A once thriving city now dying. The legacy of those captains of industry shattered. The city, county, chambers of commerce, and nonprofits crafted strategic plans in hopes for revival as early as the 1940s. But most believed the city was a relic.

I didn't hate Scranton as much as other people. Maybe it was having a poet father. I remember him telling me to always look up on the buildings. Under the grime and blight were magnificent carvings, markers of a time of affluence when the city's success seemed unstoppable. He wrote lovingly about growing up in North Scranton. He took me to Mulberry Poets and Writers readings at the Artists for Art (AFA) Gallery, an early leader in the arts scene and still thriving. Like me, he believed vacant lots could be gardens and abandoned buildings could be restaurants.

I even appreciated the seedier sides of Scranton. Eating breakfast at Tony Harding's all-night diner on Lackawanna Avenue, tucked between a pool hall and strip club, I imagined what happened the night before in the adult world. Scranton had stories, both glorious and ruinous. And I loved all of them.

I marched with my Irish dancing school in the St. Patrick's Day parade. As a teenager, my friends and I hiked up an old culm bank, a large pile of broken shale and coal dubbed "the Moon," to drink beer in red Solo cups. We sought love at church picnics on muggy summer nights, eating funnel cakes. And I can't separate my memories from networks of railroad tracks. I walked through half urban/half wilderness behind abandoned factories and convenience stores that suddenly led to the Lackawanna River flanked by raspberry bushes and sumac trees.

People asked why I moved back from California, as if this choice were a self-inflicted wound. I wasn't ignorant of the problems here. Coal mining left environmental destruction. The lack of businesses saddened me. Generations of economic loss, empty main streets, and failed political promises fostered a collective trauma. Bitterness became a protective measure against more heartbreak.

But I was surprised at an emerging sense of the possible. I attended creative gatherings hosted by a local photographer. I volunteered for community revitalization organizations. Northern Lights Café and the Espresso Bar popped up, and I wrote articles for the *Antennae*, a local zine. I forgot about future plans.

Fast forward to 2008. I find myself an arts administrator working for Lackawanna County, not something on my radar in my early twenties. But as I reflect on my time in San Diego, when I had to move a piano for an experimental performance, or when I met with a writer from Tijuana to apply for a grant to develop a US-Mexican literary festival, or even back further to the little girl dreaming of gardens in vacant lots, this fate seemed inevitable.

One of my first projects was to design a bicycle rack competition. Some people at the time claimed no one rode bikes in the city. Others believed Scranton could become a bike town. The winning design was a Gothic-style lightbulb shape acknowledging our moniker as "the Electric City" because we had the first electric streetcar. I breathed a sigh of relief when they were installed on Courthouse Square and people locked their bikes to them.

More people now lock their bikes on those racks as the city sees a rise in population and increased businesses. Public art has proliferated. County arts grants have tripled. One such grant went to the Center for the Living City, an organization celebrating the work of the pioneering urbanist Jane Jacobs, who grew up in Scranton. They created the Observe Scranton Festival based on Jacobs's principles of what makes a great city. Although the city and school district still face daunting economic struggles, there is another Scranton evolving, and it's ripe with possibility.

Some people complain that it isn't like it used to be. Some long for a time that never really existed. Politicians still campaign on a blue-collar narrative that simply isn't true anymore. If I am honest, I do worry my city might eventually lose its authenticity and displace people dedicated to it. We're beginning to discuss gentrification more than deindustrialization, as forgotten buildings transform into apartments and a culture of remote work emerges from the pandemic, making Northeast Pennsylvania an attractive place to move. But while I have loved the city even during its harder times, ultimately, a renaissance is better than decline.

Churches may struggle to hold picnics as lifestyles change, but now you can find pierogies alongside tacos in restaurants. People run on the Lackawanna River Heritage Trail alongside the Lackawanna River. The Pan-African and LGBTQ+ flags fly over city hall. My office funded a mural celebrating a vaudeville dancer, an homage to our earlier tagline, "If you could play Scranton" (meaning if the tough town of Scranton liked acts passing through, they would succeed elsewhere), but also one depicting Martin Luther King Jr. Projects with the goal to tell the neglected story of the Lenape tribe, the Indigenous people who were here first, are in motion. Neighborhoods see more civic engagement and investment.

The sun is dipping behind the mountains, and an autumn moon will soon replace it. The blood on my shin has started to scab. I'm sore and tired, but the chaos of the morning is now orderly, with tents and tables aligned and the cohesive decoration signifying harvest. The weather looks clear, and the Bonfire will be a success—as it has been in other years—bringing people from all the corners of the city to mingle and talk. Inevitably, tucked into our conversations, we'll tell stories of the city, mine among them.

Violet

JULIE ESTY

A dramatic monologue from the Dunmore Cemetery Tour

Lovely day, isn't it? The colors of autumn. Cooler days and crisp evenings are such a welcome relief from the summer months. For me this season brings with it so many memories. Some of them good—and some of them not so good. The longer evenings, more darkness, months of cold weather certainly wear out their welcome rather quickly. I think it's the darkness—the length of the days—memories lurk in the shadows waiting for their opportunity to come out of the dimness when you least expect it.

Halloween is a big occasion here in Scranton. Halloween, with its masquerade balls, was such a busy time of year for my father. I'm Violet Fahrenholt. My father, John T. Fahrenholt, was a costumer. Exciting and delightful line of work. He costumed so many in this valley for theatrical performances and parties. Everything is much more exciting in costume. Fahrenholt's was a very successful Penn Avenue business for years. The theater was a thriving enterprise here. Also, many social, religious, and fraternal organizations held masquerade parties. My father was always busy, and I have wonderful memories of him and the magical costume shop.

Of course, being surrounded by costumes, naturally, I performed regularly in amateur theater as an actress and musical soloist. I always felt that the arts—music, theater, dance—enhanced our lives considerably. I was a member of the Scranton Oratorio Society. Through that organization I met Paul. He was an Oratorio Society member. Now—there's an autumn memory. In November 1907, Paul told his parents that he had a funeral to attend up the line, and I told my parents that I had to attend a party in Old Forge. Then Paul and I boarded a train to Binghamton and acted like we didn't know each other. We certainly did. We eloped! On our return to Scranton, we kept the marriage secret. The plan was to tell everyone the following April, when we had enough money to set up housekeeping for ourselves. But I fell on an icy sidewalk in February 1908 and was badly hurt. That's when I spoke up and told my parents I was married. That marriage lasted a few years. In November 1912, Paul left me and was never heard from again. I was granted a divorce in December 1914. I never wed again. From the wonderful memories of my father's costume shop in October to Paul in November and December. Quite a shift. Even though I didn't know where Paul went, memories of him certainly came out of the shadows and raised their unpleasant head every November, lingering into December.

Four years later, in February 1918, my brother Henry died. He had tuberculosis. My mother followed him in death five months later. That same year, on December 23, my beloved father died. In one year, I lost my brother, mother, and father. That left my brother Theodore and me. Theodore suffered from addictions. Eventually, drinking took its toll, and he joined the rest of my family in December 1927.

I was on my own, and the months from November through February were always so difficult. So many memories, so many people to miss. So many times, I thought my heart would shatter into a million pieces. So many times, I wished it would. It was thirteen years until cancer claimed me and I was happily reunited with my family—in February 1940.

My advice to all is make wonderful memories with your family and friends in the midst of the wonderful fall backdrop of this valley. Enjoy the beautiful season of autumn, but be mindful that it is still a season of dying. Some of us are just trying to make it through the winter and the long, dark nights. Chill winds blowing over the windowpanes can be quite painful. Sometimes, as the earth dies, some of us die along with it.

Two poems by Scott Thomas

Three Hills

1.

Just before sunset
In the year 1962
Climb the culm bank
Like a mule
Palms wearing
A glove of coal dust
Knees blackened and bloody
When you slide.
Worth the Bactine sting
Later to watch the streetlights
Come on.
Primitive Methodist church bells
7 on Wednesdays
(Midweek Praise and Prayer)
And the fire siren every night at 9
When mother says
The sidewalks will be pulled in.
Other side of the river
Sulphuric glowing red grin
Of a newborn
Mine fire.

2.

Midday in 2.5 dimensions.
Copyright 2002 Nintendo.
Make Mario climb the hill.
Press A to jump for coins
At the crest.

Green pipes lead to coin chambers
But the ticking means the treasury
Will disappear if you are not fast.
Up button to the pipe above Mario.
Back on the sunny hill
Take care espccially
If you are low on lives
Little enemies.

3.

Before sunset
Centuries after
The Lenape lived
Where you stand,
Climb the hill of plastic,
But careful not to slip
On the Playmobil pirate ship
I assembled for my son
Christmas Day 2005—
Never asked for,
Never played with.
Step over the faded black hull;
Cannons, red sails,
Pirates with swords
Lost.
Once at the heap's summit,
Sit near an antique iMac
Careful not to cut your fingers.
Wait for night
And blackness and silence
In the valley
Except for phosphorescent toys
Glowing
Like the green campfires of refugees.
Earth once had forests
That longed for rain,
Sweet and misty

After a storm
Just as the impervious land
In your time
Needs batteries and charging stations
To come alive.
What is alive for you?
Obsolete screens glowing ill,
Indicators blinking for children long dead,
Beeps that break the birdless afternoon.
Look upon what I have made.

On Seeing Louie in a Toadstool

This one is white,
Glistening like garage sale china.
From it you can spoon the summer rain.
That one is crimson, industrial-looking,
Stamped with an illegible disclaimer.
This mushroom, dead, is wrapped in white gauze;
That one, yellow, a horizontal sun,
And over by the stump
Is a clump of orange
Shaped like cat puke.
Spend time walking among the fungi
You might be surprised
How nature stocks the forest floor,
How a mounted, gilled, fleshy disk
Shows the faded, grayscale image
Of a man on a train—
Your step-grandfather
Nearing Scranton at night, 1938.
He thinks how the lights in Lackawanna Station
Will seem so bright until he gets used to them.
Within weeks his springy flesh will rot,
But he won't care
Involved by then in an affair
With your grandmother,
A miner's wife.

Three Poems by Susan Luckstone Jaffer

Face-off at Steamtown Mall

"Don't you just love to shop?"
the woman asked, tired but happy,
designer names emblazoned like
scarlet letters on her $75 T-shirt.

The woman asked, tired but happy,
a question I had to think about.
Scarlet letters on her $75 T-shirt
swam before my eyes.

A question I had to think about—
Didn't I just love to shop?—
swam before my eyes.
I love to shop in the Salvation Army.

Didn't I just love to shop?
Well, sure—if no large bills change hands.
I *love* to shop in the Salvation Army.
Especially when there's a sale.

Well, sure—if no large bills change hands,
shopping can be fun.
Especially when there's a sale,
like when jeans are $1 a pair.

Shopping *can* be fun . . .
Like at bag sales.
Like when jeans are $1 a pair.
Like consignment shops!

"Like at bag sales?"
I asked the tired-but-startled shopper.
"Like consignment shops?"
She blinked first.

Tara Hall

I raise my glass to darkened wood, to tin
Illuminations, gummy floor, and feet
That pound and spin in crazy unison.
From arms that fall across damp necks we meet
Eyes that laugh and tear with mirth so sweet
It turns our brittle cares to powder, blown
Out the door and down the weary street.
My music swells; we've made the tunes our own.
A beer is spilled, another dart is thrown.
And in the back, scrubbed table, seating shared,
Still seasick, homesick, wetly pale, half-grown,
Four young men paint their lyrics green. Unfair
Those WASPish weekdays keep me waiting long;
I'm turned to Irish with each Saturday's song.

At Cinemark

Your glasses reflect the cinematography:
yellow one minute, blue the next.
All that stands between us is popcorn,
one buttered, one not.
Our bodies don't mark or measure
boundaries; in each other's way,
fingers lace, arms link, thighs meld.

On the screen a face, recalled so vaguely
my best guess is nameless.
"*Crossing Delancey*?" I whisper.
"Amy Irving," you whisper back. Ah.

We notice the same things. I register
the condom on the bar, the real politicians,
the fleshy softness of pregnancy, knowing
you will bring them up later, over menus.

The father says, "I have to go home."
Your hand moves to my knee. I cover it,
remembering times I had to go home.
My head drops to your shoulder
with his daughter's hurled curse.

She does unspeakable things
you and I have spoken of many times. Hands
braided in a knot, we hold on,
breathing in tandem through the credits.

Dedicated to the Venues That Raised Me

JESS MEONI

I entered high school in the fall of 2004, jazzing off of an impenetrable energy from the last summer of shows. Lights flickering, feedback blaring, piles of people pogoing, pushing, swaying, stage-diving into the crowd, releasing all uncertainty and inhibition, hoping to land on a set of hands to carry them to safety. That feeling was hard to pin words to—chaotic, invincible, reciprocal, immeasurable. There was a strong momentum of punk, hardcore, and ska bands in the Scranton/Wilkes-Barre area long built up, ever growing from past decades, and I suddenly found myself immersed in a new scene of music and art, and within this, the venues we called home every weekend.

Music was a constant for me throughout my formative years. Like many growing up in the 1980s and 1990s, I flipped through a small circuit of television channels, often switching between MTV or VH1, I frequented the Gallery of Sound and the Wall for cassettes and CDs, and I collected issues of *Alternative Press*, *Circus*, and *Spin* magazine for the latest music news. I had just turned thirteen when I began reading Jon Savage's *England's Dreaming*, a book I regarded as something of a bible at the time, and the journals of Kurt Cobain, someone I regarded as something of a savior, at least to me. Drawn to the crude, cut-and-pasted images of photocopied show flyers and the social commentary I saw within many of the books I was reading, and struggling to express myself in my newfound community, I focused all my attention on creating a preliminary cover design for *Ruthless*, my first fanzine. That same year, my friends and I formed the psychedelic garage rock band Satellite, and I joined as a drummer and vocalist. We were soon scheduled to perform our opening show at a new venue called Test Pattern located in downtown Scranton. After hearing so many stories about Sea-Sea's and Café del Sol and attending only a handful of concerts at Tink's before their demise, I saw this as a means for the next generation to make their way. I felt very drawn to this sense of punk ethos and its influence on culture and community, and now I felt that connection more than ever.

At this point, I accepted a certain reality for myself. I knew there was a negative connotation associated with Scranton. I knew people felt the area did not have much to offer. With just a limited involvement of the music scene at this age, I couldn't disagree more. Our first time playing in the basement of Test Pattern was nothing short of electrifying; total strangers took a chance on a band they never heard of and shaped our mindsets forever. For years, we played and attended countless shows at Café Metro, the Other Side, and Redwood Art Space in Wilkes-Barre; the Staircase in Pittston; and the Vintage Theatre, New Visions Studio & Gallery, the Irish Wolf Pub, and the Keys in Scranton, among many others. I saw a community not only full of potential and opportunity, but a scene that had already proven time and time again to produce lively, enriching experiences. I also came to the conclusion that the only way we were ever going to have any fun in this goddamn town was if we were going to do it ourselves.

Writing and distributing for *Ruthless*, a fanzine focused on interviews with local bands, album reviews, and art commentary, happened concurrently with my venture into community organizing. The influence of music, art, and zines of riot grrrl culture, an early 1990s underground feminist punk movement that emerged out of the Pacific Northwest, coupled with the value of creating accessible, all-ages venues, became my motivations for organizing Ladyfest Scranton. The event was a day-long music and arts festival set at Nay Aug Park celebrating local women in the scene, and it doubled as a fundraiser for the Women's Resource Center in June 2009. Almost all efforts in booking the bands and visual artists went directly through MySpace correspondence, email, or handwritten letters, and *Ruthless* acted as a vehicle to raise awareness for the event. It was a whirlwind of logistics, luck, and trial and error, but it provided the necessary groundwork for understanding the boundaries and possibilities an event could have.

The following summer, I attended the Philadelphia Zine Fest with copies of *Ruthless*. It would be my first time participating in a festival dedicated to fanzines, and I was so excited to surround myself with like-minded creators. Upon arrival, I walked inside the venue on Walnut Street and was told to just sit anywhere. I didn't find the introduction particularly warm, but I found a small available table and took my seat. Hours passed. In a room of well over twenty zinesters, practically nobody spoke to me. Even when

I tried to start a conversation myself, everyone seemed too cool for school. A rush of anxiety spilled over. I felt outcasted, intrusive, alone. I didn't belong. I left Philadelphia that day feeling defeated and confused. How could I feel this intense interconnectedness from the shows back home but feel a void when interacting with those I assumed were my peers? I took some time to think about my experience there and wondered what went wrong.

I wanted to challenge myself to turn a negative into a positive. Making zines still brought me joy. Playing in a band did as well. I saw this next step as an opportunity to improve my relationships with prospective participants in future events. There was a positive impact that could be made in welcoming each person to the event and creating a meaningful experience tailored just for that person. From there, the Scranton Zine Fest was born. Utilizing graphic design, writing, DIY ethics, and the many other skills I developed out of zine making, I was able to create outreach methods for participants from beginning to end, often mailing personalized letters, flyers, stickers, buttons, screen-printed patches, and shirts, and later, when social media became more prevalent, creating individualized posts promoting their art, writing, and music. Over a decade later, the Scranton Zine Fest is still going and has grown significantly in size and scope. I feel so fortunate to have the capability and partnerships to build a platform for cultural experiences that unify people and foster creative expression.

All in all, it was never really about the venue itself, it was about the people inside those venues that made all the difference—the people that opened their doors for all-ages events, booked your band when no one else would, let you to drop off a zine or tape up a flyer in the window. Our venues may come and go, but it's that same impenetrable energy that illuminates the next generation from a shadow of doubt.

City Noise

DIMITRI BARTELS-BRAY

I am lying in bed, attempting to nap, and I hear shouts coming through my apartment window. Fragments of sun creep in through the crannies of the blinds, and I have to focus to hear what they're saying. The first word I hear clearly is "trans," and I immediately assume people are protesting Pride Month on Downtown Scranton's Courthouse Square. The demonstrators go around the corner, and the sound dissipates, but as they return around the block, I hear what they're really saying: "Trans rights are human rights." My stomach sinks again, and I'm not sure whether to be grateful or not. Instead, I wonder if anyone will hurt the protesters.

My apartment rests on the seventh floor of a large building in Scranton's downtown, shortly past the main square. This location ensures that there is constant noise: cars honking, drunk women shouting as they stumble in heels on a Friday night, and protests, like the guy who preaches about following religion every other Saturday morning. I'm used to it, but rarely do the protests deal with anything related to me.

It's ironic because we are here; I am here. Growing up in Clarks Summit, a suburb outside of Scranton, and spending these past few years in the heart of the city itself, I have encountered dozens of members of the LGBTQ+ community, many of them also transgender. We are here, we always have been, and we always will be. Still, it's rare to really hear anything about us. Too often, we are just as invisible as we are present.

Like the intensity of the noises that I hear from my apartment, there are a lot of loud people in Scranton too, people who aren't so friendly. I think they're the reason people like me tend to be so quiet. At a certain point, there isn't a whole lot of room to be heard.

Scranton isn't unique in this aspect, but I do find it comforting that people like me are slowly but surely regaining our voices. There's still a fear there, like the fear I felt for those speaking up about trans rights, about my own rights, down the street. However, there's hope too, like the pride flags that the bar down the street hangs on its windows—and not just in June—or the fact that, somehow, I keep meeting people just like myself.

Hearing the protesters, I climb on my couch so I can peer out my window. If I get the angle just right, I can usually see the edge of the square, the intersection of the sidewalk on either side, and the statues and trees surrounding the courthouse. I catch a glimpse of a large crowd carrying papers. Someone leads the chants, but I cannot discern much from anyone's appearance. I recognize no one.

For once, I think, people like me are the loud ones.

Though I've found pride in being myself, in discovering that sense of comfort within my own skin, or at least as much as I could find considering the circumstances, it took a long time. From a young age, I had the bitter taste of the loud people in my mouth, both from teachers who were supposed to guide and protect me as well as other students. I had support as well, but it was difficult to hear when all I could focus on were the people refusing to call me by my name.

After I came out, Scranton transformed into a place where I didn't belong. There seemed to be an anti-LGBTQ+ agenda, and there was no room for people like us, people like me, to fit onto Lackawanna Avenue or within Nay Aug Park. Despite the energy and trials that it took to come out publicly in the first place, most didn't seem to believe that my efforts warranted any sort of congratulations, only thinly veiled—and sometimes blatant—hostility.

Other people within my community were out at school as well, but few were transgender, and none were widely accepted. My family, who all grew up around Scranton, were initially unreceptive too. It was only when I began a part-time job in the retail industry that I discovered a place where everyone accepted me: the Sheetz location in Clarks Summit. Over half of our workplace was LGBTQ+ in some way, and during my over five-year-long tenure, I wasn't the only transgender person either. It was a small community within a larger one, yes, but everyone was welcoming, and our voices were louder than usual.

I had planned to leave Scranton as soon as I graduated high school, convinced that the overall area would not and could not accept me, but I ended up returning to finish my degree after the onset of COVID-19. I began renting my apartment downtown, wondering if perhaps the center of the city would be more welcoming than the outskirts.

For a while, I never had that question fully answered. Yes, my university was fantastic, but what about the city itself? I assumed that I might never get an answer, but I think those protesters finally addressed my question.

Clearly, there is a vibrant community here, and, clearly, we are growing louder.

Maybe, thinking back, I have been loud in my own ways too.

In August of 2021, I began hormone therapy, the process—for me—of injecting testosterone into my body. It causes a lot of changes, such as obtaining a deeper voice, growing more body and facial hair, and overall taking on a more masculine appearance. Though the changes were initially subtle, I am now at a point where I appear very much like a man. The only issue is that, as I write this, I still have a month until my top surgery, and I have a larger chest.

People aren't sure what to assume when they look at me, confused by the mismatch of my masculine bushy eyebrows, unshaved legs, semi-longer hair, and my still-feminine large chest. Regardless of what I wish they did or didn't do, most avoid using pronouns with me, ultimately deciding it's the safer route. Sometimes, however, people do assume I am a man.

A few months ago, I left my apartment (at the time, with much longer hair), in eyeliner and with my face unshaved. It was supposed to be a way of declaring I was a man, but a man who refused to bow down to gendered stereotypes. I drove over to a local restaurant with my friend to order takeout, and the cashier stared at me as if I had grown two heads. His voice was clipped but professional, and he ended his customer service monologue with a smirk and a "thank you, *sir*." His eyes rolled as he turned to the next customer.

I didn't say anything but immediately felt my face flush and the overwhelming tinge of anxiety washing over me. My hormone therapy ensures that I cannot cry, and for once, I was grateful, as I didn't want eyeliner running down my face, disappearing into the stubble decorating the curves of my jaw.

It was an upsetting experience, and I returned home with little appetite, once again wondering why I am living in Scranton of all places. The cashier read me as a man, yes, but then demeaned me for wearing makeup on my face, for breaking gender norms. Even if I could be seen as a man immediately, I would be ostracized for my choice in fashion. There was no winning.

As I observed the retreating figures of the protesters on the square, I wondered what I was doing to be loud too. I didn't even know there was a protest scheduled—there isn't exactly a unified network for trans folks and supporters around here—but I should raise my voice too, right?

I think wearing eyeliner was my own way of doing that, of being loud.

While the LGBTQ+ community in Scranton might seem invisible, we are here. Certain people make it difficult to hear our voices. However, if silence denotes invisibility, then can it be said that, by being ourselves, we are being loud? I wore eyeliner in public, despite how it caused someone to treat me, because it made me happy and it's what I wanted to do. I am in the process of transitioning, and people aren't sure how to address me, but I continue to focus on being myself and expressing myself the way I want. Can't it be said that staying in a constant state of authenticity is one way of letting my voice be heard, of being loud?

In that case, Scranton's volume is rising and will only get higher. There is a lot of work to do, and I can't pretend otherwise. Why are people like my brother and me bullied in school? Why can't people accept others who defy the norms of clothing and makeup? Why is transgender healthcare inaccessible to so many, to people like me who are forced to drive hours away just to receive medication?

However, it's the fact that people like me and my old coworkers are no longer hiding that will help to address these questions. We seem invisible at times, but there are many of us, and we are becoming more comfortable than ever speaking aloud, not only through protests but through being ourselves every single day. Scranton is a difficult city if you're not straight or cisgender, but as people like me continue to raise our voices, I don't think that it will always be that way.

song of the city electric

ALICIA GREGA

When you find your place where you are, practice occurs, actualizing the fundamental point; for the place, the way, is neither large or small, neither yours nor others. The place, the way, has not carried over from the past, and it is not merely arising now.

—Dogen, Genjo Koan

Part 1

It took all year to write this poem.
Scranton is sensitive and I didn't want to hurt his feelings.

I hesitated to assign the city a gender
on this last day of 2022,
but there's an unmistakable whiff of testosterone in the air.
(Maybe it's the landfill.)
Feminine wiles won't get you far in this town;
it takes brawn to survive here.

Our foremothers had more to worry about than
sugar and spice and . . .
What's your definition of nice?
We honor their work once a year when we make pierogies.

Where do Scrantonians fall on the friendliness scale?
We're the punchline so often,
an easy target for elitists,
it's hard not to get defensive.
We only half-believe the hardscrabble cartoon they doodled of us.
We're allowed to make fun of ourselves;
we know how to take a joke,

but outsiders be warned—
Don't lowball the underdog.

His short commutes and deciduous refuge would be
just as loveable had I been born here instead of California.
Still, I worry my enthusiasm is Stockholm syndrome masochistic.
Why am I so loyal to Scranton?
My mother never cared for the place.

Ruthlessly pushing chicks out of the nest,
NEPA hasn't been kind to those
who chose to stay.
We the wounded, the overwhelmed, the unambitious.
Don't even think of moving back home
until you can save the rest of us.

I chose to raise my girls here
so they know where they are from.
Like antique appraisers, they know what's real.
No one moves to Scranton to become rich and famous.
It's easier to know where you stand with people.
No one hangs around in hopes you'll raise their status.

Scranton is where the rebels return
after they've brushed close enough to the stars to realize
they'll never be suitably ruthless
to sell their souls.
Integrity on one shoulder,
a chip of coal on the other.
No one cares much what you do here:
it's a blessing and a curse.

Like the best characters in every story,
Scranton has made mistakes.
In the end, we'll chalk it even.
The city gave as much as it took.
Ask the ones who've "made it there."
Life takes a toll no matter where you live.

Part 2

I told my dad I was struggling to write a poem about Scranton
and he told me to use old time sayings,
"like dupa."
We are starting at the bottom here, folx.

If I had been more callous,
I wouldn't be living with my Dad,
now, finally, at 50,
after living a lifetime of wondering what if.
He could be retired at home in Alabama
except he likes buying things,
so he reads books between check-ins at the VA,
and keeps an eye on Grandma.
Helen is so very alive at 95.

I used to think there was something wrong with me
for not wanting more, then I met my autism in a dive bar
where she knitted my broken bits together
into a tapestry of self-love.

Our ancestors brought trauma with them,
lining their suitcases with the reasons you leave.
They should have packed extra ego
to ward off Heyna accents laced with contempt.
Stacy cracked the code of Nana's letters
by reading the words phonetically in a Hungarian accent.

Their invasive seeds of doubt sown so deep,
the shame grows like dandelions,
greens no one taught us to cook,
weeds as insatiable as the slugs
who will devour your victory garden.
If the squirrels don't get there first.
The squirrels in Scranton are little assholes.

All I've been able to grow is herbs and kale.
There's not enough sun in these West Mountain foothills,

the shade of Hyde Park.
It's not that the soil is sour.
Even in Factoryville, Uncle Vince is only growing peppers this year.

The landscapers who cut down my pumpkin patch working at night
left two pumpkins on the porch after I told the landlord.
He didn't hire them back this year,
and the hedges are out of control.
There's always some guy mowing his grass in the dark.

All the secrets we think we have are the same.
We share the secret.
We are the skeletons in Scranton's closet.
You, the sacrum, the scapula;
her, the clavicle, the sternum;
him, the humerus, femur, and phalanges
over there, our skull, lacrimals leaking,
mandible flapping against the lie of time.

The House on Frink Street

DAWN LEAS

Decades-old Lincoln Logs smell
like wood right off the saw,
the new after heartbreak,
the before long silences.

A reminder of all those times
of trying to build a perfect home.
Failing one log at a time. I used
to sit on the floor for hours, days

with my sons crouched in Fisher
Price pajamas covered in trains.
One's red curls, always akimbo,
back lit by winter sun. The other's

white-blond a mess of matchsticks.
They parked cars outside our play
home while the chinking I mixed
crumbled. Wood on wood. Friction

wore me down to a nub. I chanted
(to myself, others). *Wife. Mother.*
Beyond that, *who was I?* The air
smelled of melancholy the color

of Wegman's apple juice. Not even
the red Crayola sippy cups breathed
light into the room. The tussle of boys
over a remote, explosion noises

as they kick and toss logs, opening chords
of *Thomas the Tank Engine* kept me
from demolishing the house on Frink Street.

From the Classroom to the Chaos

TOM BORTHWICK

In Scranton, not too long ago, snagging a teaching gig was like striking gold in a coal mine. It was coveted, hard to come by. But these days, a perfect storm of COVID-induced soul-searching and pitiful starting wages birthed a severe shortage of teachers, surpassing even the struggles faced by other Pennsylvania districts. During my seventeen-year career in a district just outside Scranton, I taught eleventh and twelfth graders in English, from the vo-tech kids with the best work ethic of anybody, to Mass Media in the age of disinformation (what a time!), as well as honors and AP classes.

But who the hell wants to teach these days, anyway? In this state, you need a master's degree or its equivalent every five years or else you can kiss your job goodbye. And here in Scranton, you have to dig deep into your own pockets to foot the bill for that higher education. You'll find yourself juggling the distinct personalities of 130 to 150 little devils each day, many of whom come with their own baggage of emotional meltdowns, social dysfunctions, or even legal issues. You'll be shelling out your hard-earned cash for supplies, while your pleas for reform or a helping hand will probably land on deaf ears. When my district decided to cut the librarian, then followed up by totally dismantling the library itself, what did that mean for me as an English teacher? Guess who had to spend hundreds of dollars on books for the kids? It wasn't the district.

Now, let's talk about what's in it for you. Selfish? Maybe. But let's be real. There's a golden pension waiting for you at the end of the tunnel (if you even know what a pension is these days), a decent healthcare package (compared to most poor souls out there), and a fat paycheck (once you've paid your dues in years of service). Oh, and let's not forget the feeling of imparting knowledge, experience, and wisdom to the next generation. Inspiring those little rascals to be better than those who came before. Being a rock for them to lean on. Perhaps even being the only stable force in their lives. Some of the most powerful moments for me were when a student reached out to let me know he was suicidal. The police were at my door asking questions and making sure the young man got help. (He did, and he is doing well.) Or when a student whose parent had died would just stay after school in my room to get her work done, all in the simple silence she needed. Or the multiple students who would weep or have anxiety attacks during intruder drills whom I'd take aside and comfort. And on and on. Truly, I haven't even scratched the surface of what teachers mean to our kids.

But guess what? After seventeen long years in this profession, I walked away from it all. And like some lunatic, I sprinted right back into the arms of education by throwing myself into the chaotic world of the Scranton School Board. I secured nominations from both the Democrats and the Republicans for this gig.

Though I left, it's important to say that just as I taught, I learned. I learned that seventeen years in a high school English classroom doesn't qualify me to make decisions about that classroom when a micromanaging principal who taught kindergarten for five years has better ideas. I learned that having a policy disagreement with a school director whom I campaigned with is grounds for being blocked on social media and ghosted from future policy discussions. Ultimately, I learned that power is a treacherous beast and those with it often do not like to hear a perspective other than their own. And in my time on the board, because of that power, I saw sycophants who would never have given me the time of day suddenly singing my praises. It is, I'm sure, because of this that power has a way of turning even the most levelheaded folks into egotists willing to fight battles fueled by personal vendettas with little regard to the greater good. And who suffers the most in this twisted game? Our kids, that's who.

So I am still at it, hoping to dismantle the entrenched culture of power while advocating for transparency, collaboration, and improved education in Scranton. It's a tall order, but well worth the fight.

Scranton's culture, despite its grimy power dynamics evident in corruption convictions and attention-seeking PR clowns, also boasts a glimmer of public service. If you cut through the bullshit, you'll find individuals who prioritize the well-being of the community, who strive to make a positive impact. Concerned citizens who demand transparency, digging through documents and exposing hidden truths. Moms who volunteer their precious time for the PTA. Dads who coach their kids, shaping them into future champions. Retired folks who volunteer as crossing guards and selflessly look out for our little ones. The list goes on. It's this spirit that fuels my determination to navigate the murky waters of politics and serve Scranton.

But let's get real for a moment. Breaking down the barriers that hinder progress won't be a cakewalk. By embracing a culture of collaboration, we can birth an educational system that empowers our students and lifts up our community. It might sound like a colossal feat, but mark my words, it's absolutely doable. We just need to acknowledge our past, learn from it, and avoid the pitfalls it so vividly illuminates.

In fact, I ran for the school board and won on bringing back the preschool program, restoring cuts to libraries and the arts, and stopping school closures. Guess who didn't win? Directors who stood by ending those things in the first place.

Maybe we're already learning.

Two Poems by Brian Fanelli

Walking Scranton's Streets

I think of my grandfathers
whenever I walk Lackawanna Ave
and pass markers that detail
labor uprisings,
miners shot dead.
I think of their hands,
curled around tools,
callouses and cracks
of their palms,
soot on their cheeks,
dust on their clothes.

At Courthouse Square, John Mitchell
points out, memorialized in bronze,
a labor leader needed now,
while temp agency lines
snake around corners on Spruce.

Around the corner, a Jason Miller bust,
homage to the hometown actor.
On Adams, the bar where the devil
claimed him sits cobwebbed
like the abandoned silk mills
where rats slink in shadows.

By nightfall, bars fill.
Men and women clink glasses
like my grandfathers, who left black smudges
on mugs and then slipped out to night,
slept until dawn, until another shift,
when the city's black belly swallowed their bodies.

Blaze

In Memory of Mike Ambrose

I remember you as the bearded bard,
pacing Mulberry Street outside Café del Sol,
quoting Dickinson and Mos Def in one verse,
freestyling between puffs of your smoke.
I remember your voice—
booming and whiskey-drenched,
loud like the crunch of power chords
blasting inside. You had your own crowd curbside,
fans who listened to you with the same attention
as those young punks moshing and slamming to Dead Radical,
the grindcore band your cousin fronted.
Years later, I saw you at an open mic,
still wearing a frayed hoodie and Chuck Taylors,
your brown beard thicker and longer.
You showed me a blue Bernie pin.
Only politician worth my damn vote, you said.
You read something outside that night
with autumn foliage blazing behind you,
as you spit fired lyrics about bankers, bad healthcare,
what you'd do if one day your lungs filled with tar or cancer.
When you were done, you collapsed on a bench,
catching your breath and wiping sweat.
Now I see your obituary on Facebook and read comments
praising your talent as a poet and performer.
Oh, to have heard your words again,
a Molotov cocktail against every billy club
pressed against the head of the innocent,
against every bully who called kids like us pussies for liking poetry,
or threw beer cans at us post-punk shows.
Oh, to have listened to you freestyle beneath a pale moon again
in front of some graffitied wall outside some café, your eyes fire
like that mid-October foliage when last I saw you ignite a stage.

What Washed Windows Can Do

MANDY PENNINGTON

Sometime in August 2015, I watched window washers outside the Steamtown Mall, a centerpiece of downtown Scranton. With each swipe of their sponges, I saw a bit more hope from the place.

The first glimmers that something was happening popped up a week or so prior, when my coworkers and I took our daily walk over to the Starbucks on the street level of the mall, one of the few places still open at that time. We worked across the street in the Enterprise Center, making websites, building software, and running marketing campaigns. We were well adjusted to the quiet and darkened windows on both sides of the street. But there was a flurry of activity that morning. Large wooden standees of comic book–style characters and signs appeared in the vacant store windows along Lackawanna Avenue. I don't recall the exact words, but they said something like, "Wait until you see what's coming."

Live trees replaced dead ones. Topiary bushes reclaimed planters long filled with trash and cigarette butts. A crew on ladders scrubbed the scum and filth off the windows and stainless steel around the doorways. I smiled, watching them. Because it was a step.

Four years later, I would pick up a broom and dustpan for my own life.

———

As a Scrantonian, I can tell you that recognizing that first step can be hard. If you're not keeping up with what's happening in the news (or what's happening behind the scenes, if you do some homework), you hear rumors and get your information through that lovely grapevine snaking through the Wyoming Valley. It colors your perception of what is and what could be.

"Someone bought the mall."

"I heard a real estate guy who turns buildings into lofts bought it. It'll be apartments."

"We really need a grocery store downtown. Let's hope they'll finally put one in."

"Nothing will change."

"They're gonna flip it."

"It'll be a parking lot."

"Maybe they'll turn it into a Hunger Games arena."

Those buzzings? They risk that fragile part of you that wants to be optimistic about the future of the community you live in. It's far too easy to let yourself get discouraged and sink into the warm, oppressive status quo. You begin to believe that giving in is inevitable. Someone else is always pulling the strings, right? Just stay comfortable. Don't move. After all, why risk getting disappointed when being hopeful requires effort?

———————

When I walked through the mall that August day, I felt possibilities. While far from crowded, there were people. There were signs for patrons to get easy access to wheelchairs and strollers. It looked clean. And people were talking on social media and in bars and restaurants. They imagined futures where they saw the mall as a place that wasn't falling apart but instead was bringing people together. Architects and business owners started to ask questions about what the community might look like if someone did this or that. What if this rendering became real? What if this kind of business could move into an empty space? What if we asked ourselves what we wanted Scranton to be?

What if? It's a small question. And a big one, too. It can lead to something. A raised or outstretched hand. A smidgen of effort. A changed future. Even if it's just a feeling when you're standing inside a long-neglected building, flooded with sunlight from newly washed windows.

———————

Communities experience a lot together. In the last decade? I'd say we've been through more than we ever could have imagined. We've been asked difficult questions without easy answers. How do you build something that is safe, supportive, inclusive, and equitable for all when your history warns of past corruption and broken promises? How do you get a city out of its decades-long distress and start to make it a place where people want to live, work, and worship? How do you protect your right to vote? To be who you are? To love who you love? Washing dirt off a window suddenly seems so small a thing that it doesn't really matter.

It's been seven years since I watched soapy suds run down exterior glass, cutting through the grime of years of neglect. The Marketplace at Steamtown now bills itself as a mixed-use facility. The places we always thought would make it—Starbucks and Boscov's department store—are still there. Sneaker King. The post office. Empty storefronts have been flipped to become temporary rehearsal, performance, and pop-up exhibit spaces for nonprofit organizations. A dental practice and multiple offices for healthcare groups serve a steady stream of people. You can open a phone and data plan, pay your taxes, or get a haircut. There's an aquarium and an indoor play-yard, so you'll always find families. Places to eat, learn, study, and make music dot both levels. It has become a reimagined town square of sorts that went in directions we never thought of or anticipated. It's a changed space for sure. Certainly better than what it was.

Many afternoons, my dear friend and colleague Sam and I took a walk around the Marketplace to get in our daily step counts. We'd schedule walking meetings, stride around the top level, and update each other on project statuses and goings on at the office. We actually got work done on those walks, and in the meantime, we were relieved to get away from our cubicles and conference rooms. That day in March, we leaned over the railing of the mall's upper level and looked down at the miniature figures speckling the floor below. They were buying hot lattes, bags of gummy bears from Steamtown Sweets, and new sneakers. How many were contemplating their futures? How many were worried about making the wrong decision and stood frozen in the path of possibility? I knew I had to say something. I couldn't hold it in any longer.

"I don't think I want this, Sam."

"That's completely understandable."

"I need to get out."
"I don't blame you."

I admitted it. Out loud. It was out there. I'd first come to that conclusion on a walk with my husband, Brent, in Nay Aug Park.

It was March 2019, and I was miserable that weekend. Brent and I went walking to clear my head and get me out into the fresh air, in hopes that it would lift my mood. Being shaded by trees always makes me feel better, those trunks and branches enveloping me in a sort of primal hug. Somewhere between our conversation on the trail about Easter plans and what our schedules looked like for the week, I started to cry.

Things had changed at work. The leadership role I held and the path I was on to advance to something bigger became a dead end. We had new owners. I'd have a new boss. The space I'd been given to grow and be involved in directing the company was slowly and painfully slipping away. I'd outgrown my job description, and now, I was being forced back into it. For months, I felt awful about work. I sat in meetings and wanted nothing more than to stare out the window of our conference room at people going in and out of the transformed Marketplace at Steamtown—anything other than to turn my eyes to the whiteboard that laid out the future plans of our company. I didn't want to sit on another conference call or feel my autonomy and ambition wither into a dried husk, ready to blow away in the wind. This wasn't what I wanted.

"I've gotta get out of there," I told my husband.

Sam heard me. It was time to change and seek a future that was different from the one I planned. I had to change. Perhaps that was the best thing I could have done, to look for better in the company of someone who could actually see it—when I was ready.

"I'm sorry."
"What?! Don't apologize."
"I'm letting everyone down by leaving."
"I promise that's not the case."

I stayed quiet for awhile. Just breathing. I was sweaty from walking fast, my anxiety was getting the better of me, and the heat was turned on.

Katy Perry played over the mall's sound system, and I couldn't help but think about how funny it must have been to say something so important with a soundtrack so ridiculous in the background.

"What will the team do without me?"

"We'll be fine. Don't worry about us."

"But everything I've done and worked so hard to fix, though . . ."

". . . It really doesn't matter. It's still there. You still did it. That doesn't change."

"But what am I going to do next, Sam?"

"Whatever you want. You can do anything."

"Anything. That's a big question."

———

A new and unfamiliar path emerged after I walked back to my office on Lackawanna Avenue and started drafting my resignation letter. It wasn't a path that I imagined or even one that I had considered, but it came anyway. Possibility arrived in the form of a new job offer in April, along with the opinions of others who had a lot to say about my career move.

"You're never gonna make any money working in higher ed."

"Start-up to nonprofit? That's a big change."

"Maybe you should've given the company more time to see if things got better."

"You're wasting your skills."

I left private industry for a position in higher education. I went in the direction of something that didn't just sound better—it felt better, too. Instead of selling digital marketing packages and websites, I'd be using my experience in support of a mission I believed in: learning. Even so, it was a hard and heartbreaking decision, but I don't know if change can really happen any other way. Even after my last day in the office, I carried the weight of a heavy question that still remains unanswered: "What if?"

I wonder if anyone truly knows that answer. If we ever really find out. It's in that question—with people brought together by blood, bond, or zip code—where you can dream up what better looks like and imagine your place in all of it.

You can be part of something better that doesn't just sound good but feels good. Better may start in buckets that pick up trash. In empty buildings that become mixed-use spaces. In putting in your notice because the thing you do isn't working for you anymore. Maybe a clean window is not so insignificant a thing after all. It lives in the same space where one can observe little bits of progress, like when dead plants are replaced by live ones and someone asks, "What if?"

Scranton from the Pipes

CHRIS NEWELL

On a ninety-degree Friday last August, I showed up for work at Scranton Hall at the University of Scranton. It was six in the morning, and I was greeted with the news that my partner had called in sick. That day we were supposed to finish installing a new "mini-split" air-conditioning unit in the conference room. To do so, we had to run a length of narrow diameter copper tubing through the wall from the outdoor AC unit. I've been installing mini-splits since before I could (legally) drive, but Scranton Hall was built in 1871, and the walls are thirty inches of solid granite.

My partner and I had begun the drilling the day prior, spending four hours on it and making as many inches of progress. And that was with the two of us taking turns. We'd swapped positions often, getting our entire bodies rattled by the diamond drill bit recoiling off every little imperfection in the rock. The bit got lodged in the wall every thirty seconds or so, and the angle we had to work from maximized the stress on the driller's back, shoulders, and knees. To summarize in technical industry terms, it was a "shit job."

By the end of that day, working alone, every inch of my body ached, and it felt like I was breathing through lungs full of sand. But I had drilled that hole and connected that line set.

While I stretched out on the floor, trying to straighten my spinal cord, I noticed how jarring the contrast was between the shiny white plastic mini-split and the 150-year-old stone and woodwork surrounding it. The original structure of the building was reminiscent of a time before mass-produced vinyl siding and sheetrock. The thick granite blocks that had given me so much trouble were of varying sizes and presented an uneven, rugged surface to the exterior of the building. Despite the lack of polish, the quality and experience of the masons who built it was evident in the brickwork. There was no mistaking that *people* had built it, not machines. The entire building appeared like it was built to last centuries, and at this point, it had. In comparison, the mini-split looked sterile, drab, and disposable.

Despite how jarring I find this contrast, I've never heard any of my coworkers share my misgivings. To them, the age of a building is nothing more than another complicating factor to make the job even more difficult. I think my reverence for these antiquated buildings stems from some sort of hereditary connection. My dad, grandfather, and great-grandfather, not to mention a myriad of uncles and cousins, were all pipe fitters in Scranton, so every time I rip out old work to put new equipment in, there's a decent chance it's something someone in my family installed in the last eighty or ninety years.

I don't have nearly the same aesthetic concerns about replacing pipes in some dingy boiler room as I do with more visible work like the mini-split, but the differences in how I do my job versus how my grandfather did his reflect the same changes in construction work and design philosophy as the mini-split and the granite it's mounted on. Whereas a line of copper pipe might've taken my grandfather a whole day to painstakingly braze together, fitting by fitting, I can simply use a ProPress gun to squeeze each length of pipe together in an hour with practically no skill required. With new technology like this, jobs that once would've taken years can now be completed in months, at lower cost, and with less risk to workers. I obviously can't argue with such improvements, but I do feel a hint of sadness at the lost skills and artistry of the old-timers.

In recent years, the city has begun to claw its way out of the decades-long depression since the coal mines and factories closed. Although the population is still around half of what it was in the forties, people have been moving here, and new businesses and housing have sprung up to service them, often in buildings that date back to the city's beginning. My family has been heavily involved in the renovations required for these projects, so I've spent my share of time ripping out lead pipe, pneumatic thermostats, coal furnaces, and other relics of the past. This process means a lot of "shit jobs" because of all the lead and asbestos involved and because of the lax "just get the work done" construction standards from back in the day. I've always considered today's OSHA an annoyance, but after a few buildings' worth of pipe fastened to the ceiling with nothing but tie wire and walls stuffed with old beer cans, getting yelled at for standing on the top rung of a ladder seems like a fair compromise.

It feels good to replace such hazardous material and sloppy installation with modern systems, but it almost always ends up looking, as it did in Scranton Hall, "out of place." The impressive architecture and beautiful stonework of many of the older buildings looks cheapened by modern technology. I doubt most people even take notice, but when it's something *I* installed, I find it difficult to ignore. I think my uneasiness originates, in part, because of what these renovations signify in the greater context of Scranton's future. As nice as it is to be a part of Scranton's "revival," I have doubts about all it represents.

Lackawanna County offers little for teenagers outside of aimless night drives, drug use, petty crime, and above all, complaining about our postindustrial hellhole. Most of my high school friends have left. Scranton, and Northeastern Pennsylvania in general, has suffered from "brain drain" for decades, largely due to how painfully boring it is to grow up here. The recent increase in new businesses and cultural events has mitigated the problem, but the vast majority of young people born here still move on to greener pastures at the first chance.

In high school, I was among the most outspoken of my friends hoping to move somewhere where the median resident's age didn't qualify for social security. I enrolled at the University of Pittsburgh as soon as I got my acceptance letter, unable to contain my enthusiasm at putting three hundred miles between myself and Scranton. When I got out there, though, I found it difficult to settle in. I had never realized it, but I had a deep-rooted connection to Scranton. It wasn't simply the place I grew up—it was the place my family had *built*. I actually enjoyed the short while I spent in Pittsburgh, but I quickly realized I would never feel a similar connection to any place other than that postindustrial hellhole I'd spent years complaining about. I wanted to go home and get back to building, to try and help return the city to what it once was.

Most of the people I meet nowadays are from New York or New Jersey ("front platers," as my father not-so-affectionately refers to them) and have moved here since the pandemic for the comparatively low cost of living. These newcomers are frequently young professionals with high-paying work-from-home jobs, and they are the population that many of the new businesses and residential developments cater to.

Scranton has historically been a blue-collar town, with every block boasting a bar, church, and a funeral home. Now we're getting microbreweries that charge nine dollars for a beer, hipster restaurants with Edison bulbs and uncomfortable chairs, and loft apartments with rents double the median income. Yes, these places generate jobs, but they're mostly low-paying and entry-level service work, and they don't do much to help the 20 percent of the city living under the poverty line. As more moneyed people flock to the area, the natives are getting priced out.

I returned to the University of Scranton just last week as part of a crane-lift crew to remove some old air handlers on top of Saint Thomas Hall, directly across the street from Scranton Hall. Crane lifts involve a lot of downtime, so I had plenty of time to look at the building and reminisce about drilling through that granite wall. Looking again at the building, I realized I couldn't even see any of the exterior work I'd done from the street. For all my qualms about obstructing the historic stonework with air condensers and line sets, almost nobody on campus would ever even notice they were there. I began to think that the changes in most of the old buildings I'd worked on probably went similarly unnoticed, that no one cared about old brick and mortar anymore. Whether that thought assuages my doubts about the city's future or increases them, I am still not sure.

All I am sure about is that, like the generations before me, I feel a pull to keep building and rebuilding this city that, for all there is to complain about it, sometimes seems to get it right.

The Miner

JULIE ESTY

A dramatic monologue from the Dunmore Cemetery Tour

Look around this cemetery or any cemetery. What do you see? Tombstones, monuments, flowers, and trees. The obvious. Less obvious—something you might not want to think about—mortality. Life's end. What lies ahead for you.

Every day that you wake up could be your last. But you don't really think about it. You drink your coffee and go about your day.

There were men in this valley that looked squarely at their mortality every day they went to work. The coal miners. Working every day in a subterranean hell of cold, damp, mine collapse, injuries, coal gas. Death lurked in every nook and cranny of the black underground tombs. Not only did miners look Death in the eye, but they also shook hands with him before they started their workday. Some days, Death let them pass. Sometimes he took one or two. Other days, he gathered like the farmer who harvests his fields.

My name is Anthony. Death found me in December 1914. On that day, he also claimed twelve of my friends—twelve men who I worked with. Thirteen men in one quick moment went to their eternity and other cemeteries throughout the valley when Death harvested. All thirteen gathered in one swoop on a chilly winter day at the Diamond Mine Tripp Shaft in Scranton.

Our story really starts forty years before. At the Diamond Mine in the spring of 1868, over a dozen men stepped onto the carriage that would carry them to and from belowground at the start and end of their workday. That day, the carriage broke apart. That day, men died in their descent to the underground. It was determined that the mine company was at fault due to gross neglect. But even when the mine and mine owners were at fault, they weren't. Although, after that, ten men on a carriage elevator was the maximum allowed by law. We all know that laws are broken regularly in the coal region.

Forty-six years later, I stepped onto a carriage at the Tripp Shaft of the Diamond Mine. I was joined by thirteen other men. On our descent, something horrific happened, hurling us hundreds of feet below the ground. I don't know if the carriage broke apart from age, neglect, the weight, or an explosion. In the descent, our faces were scraped off, limbs were separated from bodies, and thirteen men became an unrecognizable mass at the bottom of a mine shaft. We ranged in age from twenty-two to sixty. Death harvested. Amazingly, one man out of the fourteen of us survived by hanging on to machinery that he managed to grasp in his descent. I was twenty-two years old. Two brothers died together. Six widows were left to raise twenty-one children. One Scranton parish priest presided over a sextuple funeral. One undertaker directed a funeral cortege consisting of six hearses. One man walked away from one of the most horrific accidents in mining history in this valley and lived with that for the rest of his life.

Sometimes people would refer to those of us in the anthracite region as "just a bunch of coal miners." Coal miners—yes, we were. We were also probably the bravest men you'll ever meet. There are many who wouldn't do what we did. We faced Death every day, knowing that if he didn't get us while we worked, he would come for us later in life with every breath we took—struggling with black lung. Just a bunch of coal miners—we produced a history and heritage to be proud of, and it came on the backs of the miner.

When in Week Six a Student Spoke of Her Roommate's Father's Death

JOHN MEREDITH HILL

I told the assembled ten I'd not written
the poem I should about my brother,
his life, his death. That I felt bad about
not doing it. Maybe it meant I was
a lousy brother, so-so as a son.
I believed, I went on, I wasn't

the world's worst teacher & what
Donald Hall wrote about wanting
to produce only great poems was rousing, yes,
but working to make early drafts better
was our perhaps more attainable goal.
Then I misquoted Adrienne Rich's remark about

strong emotion & the virtue of forms
& that, I said, brings us to your response
to the worksheet & the week's prompt.
For the next two hours they determined
their sonnets, villanelles, & sestinas
showed promise. I concurred.

Some things needed attention, sure,
but they should be pumped, revved
to have new stuff to work on.
So work on it, I said.

We took a bathroom break, checked
our cells, & reconvened. When

the session at last was over, students
sauntering into the hall to a mixtape
of chair scrapes & laughter from
the room named in memory of a friend,
I sat awhile before walking to DeNaples
for a slice of pizza. Then I went home to drink.

Palimpsest of Scranton, or Scranton in the American Popular Imagination

JOE KRAUS

Ain't no party like a Scranton party, 'cuz a Scranton party don't stop.
—Michael Scott, *The Office*, season 3, episode 2

The Office's Michael Scott is supposed to make us laugh because, for all his inability to recognize his own incompetence, he actually loves where he is. He's a fool, but he's a loveable fool for the pride and affection he feels as the manager of an embarrassingly insignificant operation. "We"—that is the presumptive regular viewer—have that confirmed for us by Jim Halpert's mockery. Jim can't imagine anything worse than a life spent selling paper in a nowhere place like Scranton. And we're supposed to root for him to marry the girl at the desk across from his so the two of them can flee to the greener pastures of . . . Austin, Texas.

Everything I have I owe to this job. This stupid, wonderful, boring, amazing job.
—Jim Halpert, *The Office*, season 9, episode 25

Except, of course, even as Jim leaves Scranton in the series finale, he looks back on the place fondly. When the producers adapted the show from its British original, they looked for an American analogue to its setting in Slough, a place so notoriously devoid of culture and hope that the poet laureate John Betjeman wrote a poem calling for it to be bombed. That's what Scranton was supposed to be in *The Office*, the punchline to a joke so obvious the writers didn't have to repeat it in most episodes. A funny thing happened, though, as the show grew in popularity and its goofy office staff turned into America's coworkers: Scranton grew on everyone. People started to imagine they'd appreciate the place—maybe like the people who first found their way to it as a new city.

> *[Travelers to Scranton] will behold the hills that embosom the rich treasures of coal, and may venture (as we did) into the coal mines, under the courteous escort of Col. Scranton and Mr. Jenckes . . . Surely Scranton and the Vally [sic] of Wyoming furnish attractions for the student, who would combine pleasure with profit, equal to any that has been felt . . .*
>
> —Anonymous "traveler" writing in the *New York Times*, July 19, 1853

Look, there's a lot that's attractive about Scranton. The landscape is stunning. The rich deposits of coal and iron led to the first major steel processing venture in the country. Once that industry got going, the place mushroomed, growing from a village of 2,700 in 1850 to the thirty-fifth most populous city in the country by 1870. It drew a melting pot of mostly European immigrants, and it became a center of the railroad industry. You can stay at the magnificent depot—now the Radisson Hotel—that marked the nexus of the Delaware, Lackawanna, and Western Railroad. It's a landmark today, and it was a landmark even as the city came to develop its reputation as "the electric city."

> *The latest evidence of Scranton enterprise is shown in the equipment and successful operation of an electric street railway. This novel contribution to rapid transit has just been put in running order by the Scranton Suburban Railway Company, and moves with the regularity of clock work from the centre of the city, at a point opposite the Delaware, Lackawanna and Western Railroad station, to a suburb called Green Ridge, a distance of about two miles.*
>
> —*New York Times*, December 4, 1886

Roughly a century and a half ago, Scranton was a center of "enterprise" and innovation. Some of it we remember—like formalized industrial first aid (developed by Matthew Shields for miners in 1899) and the labor union successes that led United Mine Workers President John Mitchell to ask to be buried here—and much of it we've long forgotten. Mining called for perpetual technological advancements and, as a result, nineteenth-century engineers from Scranton filed patent after patent. We were the cutting edge, the heart of the heart of the energy sector, the Houston or Abu Dhabi of that era. The country may largely have forgotten that, but some spark of it lingers.

Once a great coal producing area, Scranton now is manufacturing everything from cigars to children's wear. Coal miners have become shoemakers, carpenters, textile weavers. Formerly unemployed diggers have found work in producing building materials, women's and children's wear, household fixtures and auto batteries.
—"1953's All America Cities," *National Municipal Review*,
Feb. 1954, p. 78

"Palimpsest" means a canvas or page that's had its original markings scraped off and written over. The original may no longer be visible, but the theory is that we can often still sense it underneath. I'd like to suggest that Scranton—or, at least Scranton in the popular imagination of America at large—is a palimpsest. Sure, we're set up to be the butt of the joke, the easy punchline, but that's because part of what makes our supposed ineptness so funny—think of Michael Scott again—is that we carry the echo of that earlier greatness. "They"—the rest of an America that doesn't know how it feels to live or work here—see us like the ex-heavyweight champion working the nightclub door or the former CEO doing "consulting" in a threadbare suit.

That place is Scranton, with clams.
—Tony Soprano, when asked what he thought of Boston,
The Sopranos, season 2, episode 1

How do you explain to outsiders what it's like to be part of this community? Tell a stranger you're from Scranton and you hear, "I've driven through there," or "my grandparents/cousins/in-laws used to live there, but they're gone," or, worst of all, "but I really like *The Office*." If all roads once led to ancient Rome, all today's roads take you away from—or possibly right past—Scranton.

*It was just after dark when the truck started down
The hill that leads into Scranton Pennsylvania.
Carrying thirty thousand pounds of bananas.*
—Harry Chapin, "Thirty Thousand Pounds of Bananas"

It can get apocalyptic. Hugo Award–winning science fiction author James Blish wrote a series of "Cities in Flight" novels about an interstellar economy where entire Earth-based cities launched themselves into space and served as roving labor for the extraterrestrial colonies of the rest of the galaxy. As he imagined it, we were the worst of the worst.

> *Scranton had become steadily greedier as the money to be made dwindled, but somehow never greedy enough. Now, as it had for so many other towns, the hour of the city's desperation had struck. It was going into space to become a migrant worker among the stars.*
> —James Blish, *A Life for the Stars*, 1962

And it can get mean. Funny, maybe, but mean.

> *I come from Scranton, Pennsylvania, and that's as hardscrabble a place as you're going to find. I'll show you around some time and you'll see. It's a hellhole, an absolute jerkwater of a town. You couldn't stand to spend a weekend there. It's such an awful, awful, sad place, filled with sad, desperate people with no ambition. Nobody, and I mean nobody—but me—has ever come out of that place. It's a genetic cesspool. So don't be telling me that I'm part of the Washington elite because I come from the absolute worst place on earth: Scranton, Pennsylvania.*
> —Jason Sudeikis as Joe Biden on *Saturday Night Live*, Oct. 4, 2008

Or sometimes mean without the funny. Richard Stark's series of best-selling Parker novels told the exploits of a hard-boiled professional thief who goes up against the Mafia and the established elite, stealing and killing as necessary. At the end of the third novel, he reflects that he likes to celebrate a successful job with random sex. As he lies low in Scranton for a couple days, though, the only accessible woman is the hotel housekeeper, whom he assumes must have a "bovine mind" behind her bovine face. He ends the novel deciding, literally, that he does not give an *[expletive deleted]* about Scranton.

> *Tonight, maybe he'd go down into Scranton, though he'd never found much worthwhile in Scranton. If not, he could wait 'til tomorrow night. That Harrow could take care of things. He could save it 'til then. The first one after a job ought to be a good one, like Bette, not a pig from Scranton.*
> —Richard Stark's *The Outfit* (1963),
> No. 3 in the Parker series, chapter 22

But it doesn't have to stay dark. That's the nature of a palimpsest; it's one story etched atop another, none quite erasing the other. If you've spent time here, and if you can see that the way the country imagines this place carries a dash of envy alongside the mockery, it's all the easier to celebrate.

> *Coach: Oh, Christ, boys, Christ, it's so good . . . the joy in my heart to feel you around me again, together again, can't find words to say it . . . Magnificent! My boys standing around me again! A toast to the 1952 Pennsylvania State High School Basketball Champions! You were a legend in your time, boys, a legend. Never forget that, never.*
> —Jason Miller (Academy Award– and Pulitzer Prize–winning
> Scranton native and graduate of the University of Scranton),
> *That Championship Season*, Act I, p. 17

You can take the boy out of Scranton, but you can't necessarily take the Scranton out of the boy. Literary critic, poet, and novelist—what the Europeans used to call a *belletrist*—Jay Parini has written a number of terrific books about his native city. In his recent memoir about his friendship with the famous writer Jorge Luis Borges, he recounts thinking that he might have to flee the country to escape the Vietnam draft.

> *I could become a Canadian, as they apparently welcomed draft resisters. This would, however, put me outside my American world forever. I would become a true alien not just an inner émigré. And this frightened me, as I loved my family, even Scranton, with its familiar landscape and rhythms, a feeling of home that is impossible to find just anywhere.*
> —Jay Parini, *Borges & Me*, chapter 14

And maybe University of Scranton President Scott Pilarz, SJ, summed it up when, as he helped oversee plans for the DeNaples Student Center, he proposed a quote from the Jesuit poet Robert Southwell. He wanted it to be carved into the concrete of the new building as a perpetual directive to the university community: "Don't waste love," in particular the love you'll know in your time at Scranton.

> *Not where I breathe but where I love, I live.*
> —Robert Southwell, SJ

And that, in less poetic fashion, turned out to be the point of *The Office*. We have been a center of innovation, and we have been a handy image for postindustrial blight. We have seen much of our infrastructure rot, and we've turned out a president. We have written one story on top of another, mixing electricity with torpor, moving on through more than a century and a half of American history as a symbol of extraordinary highs and embarrassing lows. In the end, it's less about how the rest of the country sees us (though, let's face it, we're vain enough to appreciate the attention) than it is about the everyday experience of living in a city filled with capable, distracted, healthy, sickly, homely, beautiful, creative, bored, hungry, and fulfilled people. It's about living our own lives inflected by this place we've come to find as our shared home.

> *All in all, I think an ordinary paper company like Dunder Mifflin was a great subject for a documentary. There's a lot of beauty in ordinary things. Isn't that kind of the point?*
> —Pam Beasley Halpert, *The Office*, season 9, episode 25

Contributors

Amye Archer is the author of *Fat Girl, Skinny* (2016) and the coeditor of *If I Don't Make It, I Love You: Survivors in the Aftermath of School Shootings* (2019). She is a mental health writer and host of the podcast *Little Miss Recap*. You can learn more at www.amyearcher.com.

Dimitri Bartels-Bray is a senior at the University of Scranton studying English and political science. He is interested in environmental policy and hopes to pursue a career in the field, though he intends to continue writing fiction and creative nonfiction whenever and wherever possible. Currently, he lives in Downtown Scranton, where he collects books, blankets, and *The Office* paraphernalia.

Thomas Kielty Blomain is author of three poetry books: *Gray Area* (Nightshade Press), *Blues from Paradise* (Foothills Publishing), and *Yellow Trophies* (New York Quarterly Books); editor of *5 Poets*; and coeditor of *Down the Dog Hole*, collections from Nightshade Press/Keystone College Books. His poems appear in a number of anthologies, including *Coalseam*, *Palpable Clock*, and *Pennsylvania Seasons* (University of Scranton Press); and *Common Wealth* (Penn State University Press). He also writes stories and songs and plays pretty good guitar. A lifelong resident of Lackawanna County, he lives in Scranton's Hill Section with his wife, Jessica.

Tom Borthwick makes hard cider for a living at Electric City Ciderworks in Old Forge, Pennsylvania. Before that, he spent many years as an English teacher and adjunct professor. He is an MFA graduate of Wilkes University, where his mentor was author Kaylie Jones. He lives in Scranton, Pennsylvania, USA. His work has previously appeared in *Perihelion*, *Phanataxis*, and alongside Hugo and Nebula Award–winning authors in the cyberpunk anthologies *Altered States* and *Altered States II*.

David Elliott is the author of three books of poetry: *Though the Silence*, *Wind in the Trees*, and *Passing Through*. For twenty-five years, he worked with the Friends of the Scranton Public Library to bring major American poets to read in Scranton. His long involvement with Mulberry Poets and

Writers included serving on the board for many years. He is professor emeritus at Keystone College, where he taught creative writing, literature, and the history of jazz.

Julie Esty, a lifelong Scrantonian, wears many hats (and costumes!). She is the creative director for the Dearly Departed Players, a costumer, historical interpreter, author, photographer, taphophile, and—most importantly—a mom. According to Julie, cemeteries are like libraries with so many great stories—and it's her job to find and tell them!

Brian Fanelli, a Scranton native, spent his teenage years going to local punk rock clubs, including Café del Sol, Café Metropolis, and others. He eventually moved to the Philly area and then bounced back to NEPA, where he currently resides with his wife, Daryl, and their cat, Giselle. His latest book is *Waiting for the Dead to Speak* (NYQ Books), and his writing has been published in the *LA Times, World Literature Today, Paterson Literary Review, Pedestal*, and elsewhere. Brian also loves horror movies and is a contributing writer to HorrorBuzz.com, *Signal Horizon Magazine*, and 1428 Elm. He has an MFA from Wilkes University and a PhD from SUNY Binghamton University. Currently, Brian is an associate professor of English at Lackawanna College.

Daryl Fanelli is the author of *Synonyms for (OTHER) Bodies* (NYQ Books). Her poetry has appeared in *Diode, Poet Lore, Harpur Palate*, the *American Journal of Poetry, Best American Poetry Blog*, and elsewhere. When she's not writing, Daryl likes to curl up with a good book, watch a spooky movie, strike a yoga pose, or dance the night (or day) away.

Gerard Grealish, born in New York City, considers Scranton to be at the heart of his life. He first came to Scranton to attend the University of Scranton, where he obtained two degrees. Later, after founding the Mulberry Poets and Writers Association, he traveled to Alaska, where he worked in fisheries, and then to Europe, where he taught at the University of Maryland European Division. Upon attaining his law degree, he practiced criminal defense law in Scranton for years. His book of poems, *The Calculus of Imaginaries*, was published by NYQ Books in 2020.

Alicia Grega, a resident of Scranton's Hyde Park neighborhood since 1999, enjoys sharing her passion for the arts and storytelling with students and audiences of all ages. She has taught courses at Lackawanna College, Wilkes University, and the University of Cincinnati, and worked as a journalist at the Scranton Times-Tribune's *Electric City* for fifteen years.

John Meredith Hill, a graduate of the Iowa Writers' Workshop, lives on Cape Cod with Ann Maxwell Hill and a dog named Larkin. He is professor of English emeritus at the University of Scranton.

Maria Johnson moved to Scranton in 1996, which means at the time of printing, she will have lived there for very nearly half her life. She teaches theology/religious studies at the University of Scranton and is working on a MS in Counseling. She is the author of *Strangers and Neighbors; What I Have Learned about Christianity by Living among Orthodox Jews* and *Making a Welcome: Christian Life and the Practice of Hospitality*, but will only *really* consider herself a writer if she manages to complete a novel.

Joe Kraus is a professor at the University of Scranton in the Department of English & Theatre, where he teaches American literature and creative writing. He is the author of *The Kosher Capones* (Northern Illinois UP, 2019), and his creative work has appeared in the *American Scholar, Riverteeth, Under the Sun*, and the *Baltimore Review*, among other places. He is a two-time Pushcart nominee, has been long-listed for *Best American Essays*, and won the 2007 *Moment*/Karma Foundation International Short Fiction Contest.

Susan Luckstone Jaffer is originally from New York City, but she is a longtime resident of rural Pennsylvania. Her poetry has been published in *Yankee, America, Potato Eyes,* the *Lyric, Light*, and others, including the anthologies *Palpable Clock* and *Down the Dog Hole*.

Dawn Leas is the author of two chapbooks, *A Person Worth Knowing* and *I Know When to Keep Quiet*, and a full-length collection, *Take Something When You*. She's a writing coach, manuscript consultant, and arts educator. She's also a back-of-the pack runner, newbie hiker, salt-water lover, and mom of two grown sons.

Stephanie Longo is a native of Dunmore, Pennsylvania. She is the author of three books on NEPA's Italian American history and is currently a doctor of strategic communication student at Regent University.

Ted LoRusso's plays have been produced in Manhattan and across the United States, Canada, and maybe Taiwan. He won the Venice International Film Festival's "Critics' Choice" Award for Best Screenplay and the New York City Underground Film Festival's "People's Choice" Award for his feature film *Cracking Up*. His lyrics for "Attack of the Rock People" can be heard on Norah Jones's indie-rock album *El Madmo*. Mr. LoRusso is the only waiter to be knighted by the Blues Brothers Band. He prefers to be called "Sir Ted," and a curtsy won't go unnoticed.

Bonita Lini Markowski lives with her family and three cats and teaches in Northeastern Pennsylvania. She received her MFA from the Rainier Writing Workshop at Pacific Lutheran University. Her work has appeared in *Gyroscope Review* and *Sonic Boom Journal* and is forthcoming in the anthology *The Power of the Feminine I*. Her work has been chosen for Poetry in Transit for Luzerne County, Pennsylvania.

John (Jack) E. McGuigan is a retired secondary school English teacher and was a rostered poet with the Pennsylvania Council on the Arts conducting poetry residencies in over fifty schools. He is the author of two books of poetry, *Part of a Geography* and *A Wonderment of Seasons*.

Maureen McGuigan is the Lackawanna County director of arts and culture. She served as rostered poetry and playwright for many years with the Pennsylvania Council on the Arts and holds an MFA in creative writing from St. Mary's College of California. You can read her blog at CellarFive.com.

Jess Meoni, a mover and shaker from Northeast Pennsylvania, creates platforms and programs for communities by implementing her skills as a graphic designer, organizer, photographer, writer, and educator. She is involved in making zines, self-publishing her music, and activism work since 2008, and is credited with establishing the Scranton Punk Rock Flea Market and Zine Fest in 2010. Since then, Jess has launched several successful TEDx Talk conferences and the all-women open mic known as Grrrls Night, and she also became the cofounder of Second Banana Co., an alternative textile business that creates patches, buttons, stickers, and more. Her influences derive from all things rebellious and embellished— eccentric rock 'n' roll album art, kitschy twentieth-century store signage, and vintage novelty toys and trinkets, as well as 1960s sci-fi and horror comics. Jess received her bachelors of fine art in 2012 and her masters of fine art in 2015, both in graphic design from Marywood University. She currently works and lives in Scranton, Pennsylvania.

Sondra Myers has been a citizen of the world, working on behalf of civil liberties, economic justice, and the humanities in political appointments ranging from Harrisburg to Washington, DC, and Rwanda. She has chosen to live in Scranton, though, raising her family here, developing the Schemel Forum, and contributing to the cultural life of the city in countless ways. She shares her thoughts on a place that has been her home for decades. Sondra has said often that she set out to "bring the world to Scranton," and in a life spent in the service of both culture and politics, she has done as much to accomplish that as anyone.

Chris Newell is a senior English major at the University of Scranton. When not working at his family's construction business based in Throop, he spends his free time wandering the wooded hills of Northeastern Pennsylvania hunting, fishing, and flipping over rocks to look for salamanders. He currently resides in his great-grandfather's home in the Bellevue neighborhood of the west side of Scranton.

Pauline Palko splits her time between Scranton, Pennsylvania, and her home sheltered in pastoral Northeast Pennsylvania, where she finds inspiration from both the seasonal cycles of nature and the bustle and cultural influences of the many people she meets and works with. An enthusiastic Anglophile (it must be something in her DNA), she loves a good strong cuppa and a scone in the afternoon and is working up the nerve to try making her own clotted cream.

Janvi Patel is a full-time Indian American and philomath who enjoys exploring her perspective and perception of the world as a woman, writer, and Indian American. In her free time, she watches movies and shows in multiple languages while analyzing and learning about psychology, cultural and/or social issues, and scriptwriting. At bedtime, she googles things like: Who excluded Pluto from the planets? As a student at the University of Scranton, she aspires to write and experience multiple opportunities in writing, including (but not restricted to) novels, scriptwriting, and poetry.

Mandy Pennington is a writer, marketer, and teacher with a passion for storytelling. She lives in Scranton with her husband, Brent, and two mischievous cats. Mandy is also currently pursuing her MFA in the Maslow Family Graduate Program in Creative Writing at Wilkes University.

Lizzy Ke Polishan is the author of *A Little Book of Blooms* (2020). Her poems have recently appeared or are forthcoming in *PRISM International*, *RHINO Poetry*, and *Psaltery & Lyre*, among others. She lives in Pennsylvania with her husband and their cat Herman.

Laurel Radzieski is a poet and the author of *Red Mother* (NYQ Books, 2018), which won the 2020 Whirling Prize in Poetry. Her poems have appeared in the *New York Quarterly*, *Rust + Moth*, *Atlas and Alice*, on a street sign in Wisconsin, and elsewhere. She earned her MFA at Goddard College and lives in Southeastern Pennsylvania. Laurel can be found online at www.laurelradzieski.com.

Andrea Talarico is a Brooklyn-based writer, poet, and editor. In 2003, Paperkite Press published her chapbook, *Spinning with the Tornado*, and Swandive Publishing included her in the 2014 anthology, *Everyday Escape Poems*. During her years living in Scranton, Pennsylvania, she ran Anthology New and Used Books, hosted poetry readings, and penned a literary arts column for *Electric City* magazine. Her work has appeared in the *St. Mark's Poetry Project*, *Luna* magazine, *Brokelyn*, *Yes, Poetry*, and others.

Barbara J. Taylor, a novelist who was born and raised in Scranton, Pennsylvania, sets her stories in the hometown she loves and populates them with miners, evangelists, vaudevillians, gangsters, seers, and a prostitute or two. She is the author of *Sing in the Morning, Cry at Night*, and *All Waiting Is Long*. Her latest book, *Rain Breaks No Bones*, the final installment in her Scranton trilogy, is set to be released in the spring of 2024.

Scott Thomas has a BA from Bard College, an MS in library science from Columbia University, and an MA in English from the University of Scranton. He is the chief executive officer of the Scranton Public Library. He is also an adjunct faculty member at Northampton Community College. His work has been published in *Mankato Poetry Review*, the *Kentucky Poetry Review*, *Sulphur River Literary Review*, *Webster Review*, *Poetry East*,

Stirring: A Literary Collection, Poem, Philadelphia Stories, Poetry Bay, Floyd County Moonshine, Talking River, Pointed Circle, Plainsongs, Ship of Fools, Think, Spoon River Poetry, and other journals. He lives in Dunmore, Pennsylvania.

Jade Williams is originally from the Hill Section of Scranton and now resides in the Midwest. She is currently a PhD candidate at the University of Illinois at Urbana-Champaign, studying contemporary Black literature with a focus on pleasure and sexual politics. Her writing and research centers personal narrative and the transformative power of intimacy.